My Life

Scientist and Entrepreneur

By

William David Unsworth

Copyright William David Unsworth © 2019

Ultimate Publishers, Warrington, UK.

bil@unsworth.com

ISBN 978-0-9558562-1-1

Library of Congress Control Number:2019912678

First Edition – August 2019

Also by William Unsworth:

Sail on Silvergirl – Diary of Jennifer Holly Unsworth (née Stephens), 1946–1971. ISBN 978-0-9558562-0-4

Introduction

When my father was nearing the end of his days, he said that he was writing the story of his life. I came to read it after he had passed away and found that it started with an account of the arrival of the Anglo-Saxon people's into England and the origins of the surname Unsworth. This was very interesting and it went into some detail. Unfortunately that was all there was. So there was nothing about his life, growing up before the war, working during the war and his subsequent career and family. This was a big disappointment. So I have decided to put down the story of my life (and I will share the very few memories I have of what he told me about his life).

Apparently, according to Jeremy Lewis who wrote obituaries for the *Telegraph* and was editor of the *Oldie* magazine, everybody lies in their autobiographies (and in the obituaries they submit "in advance"). You want to provide an interesting narrative including important occurrences but do you want to offend anybody? What about family, ex-colleagues, ex-lovers and ex-wives. If it is to be truthful and complete I suppose all the above. People scan accounts of this type to see what is said about them and get upset – usually because they only merit a few words. I have decided to take a bit of a middle path by terminating the account after I retired. Plenty has happened since, so maybe there will be a second edition when a few more people have died. So apologies if you don't get a mention!

Early Life

I was born in Jericho hospital just outside Bury, Lancashire. My father Fred was an engineer and 20 when he had me. My mother Marian Bailey was a bit older. I believe that they first lived with my paternal grandfather, Albert Unsworth, in Bury in a house, since demolished, 51 Irwell Street. They bought a house, 321 Dumer's Lane, Radcliffe quite soon after with a mortgage from his trade union. This house still exists and I have looked at it on Google Maps. According to my National Identity Card, I was registered as being there in May 1947. I was baptised at St Marks Church, Dukinfield on 4th August 1946. My god parents were my uncles Wilfred Bailey and William Buckley and my aunt Edith Buckley. Also recorded on that certificate is a note of my date of confirmation, June 1947.

I do remember a little bit about living in Dumer's Lane. For example, the house had an internal glass door and I remember there was some anxiety about it breaking and hurting someone. It had a small back yard that opened out onto an alleyway. The front garden had a lawn and I remember sitting on this lawn feeling the grass and being a bit amazed by it. The grass was at the stage of sending out shoots to seed and I ran my hands through it.

I started school from there, and I went to Radliffe Hall Junior School, Bury Road, which was nearby. I vaguely remember that it had a wall of red stone blocks around the playground. I have a memory of walking back to the house on a hot summer day, crossing a bridge over a river (probably the River Irwell) and feeling very tired, scuffing along making a trail in the sand. I was told later that my mother used to like to walk me over to see my Aunty May who lived nearby. My father used to buy sweets for us on a Friday night; he was paid cash once a week. I liked the Cadbury's Crunchie bar.

They talked about the winter of 1947, which was very harsh, and they used my pram to go and collect some coal to heat the house. My sister was born 13th June 1951, and July 1951 we moved to 139 Cheveral Avenue, Coventry.

Mother and Father

I need to digress to give some information about my mother and father. My father was born in Bury on 9th June 1925. He had two older sisters, Marion and May (who liked to be called Jean). His mother had died young – ill from an infected cut (apparently after blacking a grate), which left her an invalid, and then subsequently she fell into an open fire in the house. He must have been bright because he went to the local grammar school leaving quite early (14 or 16?). He recalled having broken his ankle as a child – he was spinning around on one foot and his foot got stuck in a crack in the pavement.

His father Albert got him an apprenticeship with a local engineering firm but he got into trouble and was fired after an incident involving an initiation ceremony for a new apprentice. However, he must have got another post and eventually became an engineer. He tried to get a place to study engineering at Manchester University. He knew he had failed to get the place after they asked him what newspaper he read, and he said *Daily Mail*. I think that he had a bit of a chip on his shoulder about that and in later life (in his 60s) he applied for and got a place at the Open University but didn't take it up – the offer was enough.

He was a keen cyclist and used to race at Fallowfield in Manchester. The last bike he bought was a very sporty Claude Butler but I am not sure that he ever raced that bike. During the war he was selected for officer training. However, he was deemed necessary to the war effort and wasn't allowed to join up.

He worked in Trafford Park (the first industrial park built in the UK – now more associated with the Trafford Centre shopping mall). In his garage he had some bits of duraluminium from the time he worked there – it was a strong aluminium alloy used in the production of aeroplanes and I am sure he said the bits were from a Lancaster bomber.

He met my mother Marian Bailey (born 22nd January 1923) during the war. She and her sister Edie were keen cyclists and I think he met them out cycling. He helped them out when they had a puncture. They later met up when the two sisters and their mother stayed in Higher Whitley in Cheshire for a holiday. They recalled the area quite well on a visit to us in the 80s. They couldn't identify the actual house they stayed in.

They often reminisced about cycling holidays during the war in the Lake District, staying in youth hostels and, on one occasion, taking their bikes over Black Sail Pass. I have walked it a few times and they would have had to carry their bikes. The YHA hostel there is well known but very basic. They were disappointed in much later years to go back and find the Lakes very crowded! There are photos of me playing in a stream in the Lake District aged 4 or 5. One time my Dad lifted me up and put me on a wall. I said I could get down by myself and jumped. Unfortunately I didn't jump out far enough and scraped the back of my legs against the stones of the wall and did I howl. You would think that would have taught me to look before I leapt because, whilst at junior school in Coventry, I jumped backwards off a climbing frame and managed to hit my jaw on a lower strut. Fortunately my tongue was not out and I didn't lose any teeth.

My mother had lived in Railway Street, Dukinfield (the house now demolished) and she went to St Mark's primary school. Edie, her sister, was a few years older than her and apparently, she used to follow Edie to school (while she was too young to be admitted herself). They kept on taking her home but, in the end, they just let her sit at the back of the class. She went to the local secondary school and left to go to work. The family was rather poor and her father had been out of work for many years in the period before the war during a crisis in the cotton industry. There was also a brother – Wilfred Bailey. I believe that she worked in a munitions factory during the war.

My parents got married on 1st September 1945 just after the war ended.

Coventry

My father lost his job in Bury and was out of work for a bit. He then got a job in Coventry and hence we all moved. The house was a pre-war terraced house with three bedrooms, sitting room, front room and kitchen with an upstairs bathroom. The bath had a frightening gas boiler that had to be lit – it made an awful bang and made a lot of noise when burning. The sitting room had some French windows leading to a garden with grass. The kitchen was built out from the back. It had a water tank on the kitchen roof. There was a concrete path to the back gate which opened onto an alleyway that was wide enough to just drive a car down. The garden had a couple of mature trees – a rowan and a silver birch. Kids used to come to the back gate on the alleyway to listen to me swearing. The funny thing about this memory is that neither I nor my parents have been much into swearing.

My father built a brick garage at the end of the garden. This involved the felling of the silver birch, which quite upset me at the time – I have tended to plant a silver birch or rowan at each of the houses I have lived in. My recollection is that he bought a car sometime after he had built the garage. However I think he bought the first car they had (a Standard 12) only when he had got a job in Bedford (see later), which seems a bit inconsistent to me now. Maybe he built the garage in anticipation of getting a car?

My sister Margaret was born on 13th June 1951 and it must have been just before we moved to Coventry, but I have no recollection of her as a small baby. She only entered my consciousness as she became a toddler.

I started at Hill Farm Junior School after the move to Coventry. I was only there a short time before moving to a newly built school – Radford Primary. I do however vaguely remember Hill Farm. I am sure that in the first term/year we would have a lie down in the afternoon. I also remember that one of the things we did was to take in some milk and use it to try and make butter and cheese.

So I must have been six or seven when I went to Radford Primary school. I walked to the school each day by myself either down Cheveral Avenue and Bede Road or behind the cinema. I got into quite a lot of trouble at the school at first.

They thought I was a bit stupid because I had difficulty reading and learning to tell the time. I was put out in the corridor underneath a clock and told to stay there until I could tell the time. On another occasion I was locked in a school cupboard after the class teacher got fed up with me. She called the fearsome headmistress. She used to clench her teeth and shout.

Whilst at Radford I obtained a swimming certificate from the City of Coventry for doing one length of breaststroke (July 1957).

My mother and father then got involved. One evening he started to try and get me to read the words from his newspaper. He got irate and then suddenly said – "he can't see the letters". I was short-sighted and really hadn't twigged to what was going on with the vague squiggles I was expected to recognise. I don't know why this was a surprise to them because my father always wore glasses. So off to the opticians and, lo and behold, I advanced rapidly at school albeit from a delayed start. I became an avid reader and would ride on my bike to the library at Jubilee Crescent and read like mad. I started with the children's selection but soon became interested in history and all kinds of adventures. The William books by Richmal Crompton struck a chord and I used to laugh out loud at the antics of the Outlaws and their dog Jumble.

One thing puzzled me for quite a while when reading history. Who were the Byzantines? There were the Greeks, then the Romans and then the middle-ages with English Kings and the Norman Conquest – but where did the Byzantines fit in? Eventually I realised that they were the eastern successors to Rome once the Empire became split into East and West.

I was sent every so often to a barber's opposite the cinema on Radford Road and paid sixpence for a short back and sides. My mother must first have taken me of course. This was in a line of shops. I would go into a paper shop to buy my favourite sweet – a toffee cup – on my way to school. One year after the summer holidays my mother sent me to school a week too soon! At that school and also living near me were a couple of friends – Stephen Wilson being the one I remember most. He used to delight in getting me into trouble.

One year I was thrown out of the Christmas show. A highlight was a medieval pageant with a roasted pig's head carried down through the audience. He got to carry the pig's head and, for some reason, I was taken out of the show. He lived in a large house further up Cheveral Avenue towards Coventry. He was an only child and had a dog. One day we were out on the opposite side of the road and I called the dog to us. A car came round the corner and the dog was killed. He always blamed me for that. He got me into some more serious trouble in my last year at Radford. I was with him walking back and he followed a girl from our class and asked her to show him her knickers and more. I was really just there with him. Of course there were consequences and the girl's parents came round to my house (and to his) to complain. My mother saw them and was pretty upset and sent me upstairs to await the arrival of my father. I expected the worst. He had had his slipper to me a few times whilst we were in Coventry. He would clench his teeth with his lower teeth forward over his upper teeth and shout. He had got very upset with me over my difficulty in tying my shoe laces once and smacked me. I can't remember the other causes of his anger. However in the case with the girl he and my mother talked to me and emphasised the potential seriousness of what we had done. It was enough to put an innocent young mind off girls indefinitely.

We had friendly neighbours – The Wilkinsons – Alf and Nellie. They had a son, John, who was older than me and a girl, Joy, who was a year younger than me and who also went to Radford primary. Joy was always round at our house and she appears in a number of the family photos from that time. The 1950s were a time of growing prosperity and we had a television set at the time of the Coronation – 1953. We got together with the Wilkinsons at Christmas and, one year, my father bought us a Monopoly set and we played it with them next door. I particularly remember one year when it snowed on Boxing Day and we ventured out in the snow to go next door. The Wilkinsons made their own Egg Nogg each year and my mother always enjoyed an Advocaat, whether from that time or because she had had it before.

I received a range of Xmas and birthday presents. One year my father made me a pinball set out of wood with steel ball bearings to be flicked around. I was playing with a ball bearing one day, lying on my back and dropping it into my mouth. Of course one went to the back of my mouth and I had to swallow it. Panic ensued and I was rushed to the doctors who told them to just let it pass.

My father also made a sledge for us, which we had for years. I remember it being used after we had moved to Bedford – maybe it was made in Bedford? It never worked very well and would not glide along. I don't think he understood the principle of a sharpish blade melting the ice as it passed over it and lubricating the movement. It had wide flat blades. The oldest item I have from that time is a small wooden Bermuda rigged yacht, which has a solid hull. I found out online that it was a Star Yacht made by a company based in Birkenhead that had been very successful after the war. After I had left home it must have got knocked about and my father repainted it for my nephew Alex Cooper. One year I was given a bow and arrow. It was quite large and had a metal bow riser (the part that the string is attached to at both ends) and, unfortunately, it broke quite quickly, which was perhaps just as well. He had produced a target with bull's eye and roundels to go with it.

I was given a tent one birthday. I was putting it up by myself in the garden and John Wilkinson called to me over the fence. He was a scout so he knew what he was doing, didn't he? He told me to tighten up the guy ropes which I did a couple of times. He insisted that they should be tighter and then – rip – too tight and the fabric at the metal ring where the poles went ripped. I was horrified and upset and looked round to find that he had scarpered. An early lesson in not to trust people too much and the advantage of understanding things yourself rather than relying on others!

We went to the Lake District one year by bicycle. My father had modified a tandem so that I could sit on the back seat with special peddles higher than normal so that I could reach them and help with the effort. On the back of the tandem was a child seat for Margaret. The tandem had two sets of brakes and Derailleur gears. I seem to recall that one set of brakes (both were for front and back wheels) was actually a hub (disc) brake rather than the more normal callipers. My mother had her own bike.

We stayed many times at a B&B in St Johns Vale, near Keswick, run by a Mrs Thompson. The house is still there, set back on

the right as you go north after leaving the main road to
Keswick. Mr Thompson was a forester. There was a large
working horse in the field at the end of their drive. They
persuaded my grandmother and grandfather Bailey to go and
stay there one year. They said it was the only time they had
been to the Lakes, although they had had holidays in
Blackpool, and greatly enjoyed it. He liked to walk down to the
Kings Head for a beer in the evening.

It was hard work on the bike and I am not sure I really pulled
my weight all the time. The pass of Dunmail Raise presented
something of a problem as it had to be traversed to go to the
north Lakes from Grasmere. He needed all four brakes to slow
us down as we descended. Disaster struck on the way home.
Something broke on the tandem. I can't remember what but it
was not readily repairable and we ended up stuck in Uttoxeter.
They had very little money left but managed to scrape enough
together to get the train back to Coventry. We must have
walked home from the station.

Sometime after this holiday they had something of a financial
crisis, over what I do not know. They persuaded me to let them
have the contents of my Post Office savings account, which
mainly consisted of money given to me by grandparents, aunts
and uncles for birthdays. I had been saving hard and there was
about £30 there. In return I was going to get my mother's bike.
I was just about large enough for an adult bike. It was a red
racing bike (with a cross bar) and dad must have done a few
modifications to it for me.

I was entered at 11 for the entrance exam to the grammar
school, King Henry VIII in Coventry, but I failed to get in.
Stephen Wilson did pass, however, so we went to different

schools. I was not bothered as I felt that he had dropped me in it too often by then and didn't like him that much. I went to Barkers Butts Secondary Modern School, which was known as a tough school. On one occasion that first term Stephen came down on a bike one evening to see me. I was playing with other boys and we started racing on our bikes. We thought it great fun to ride alongside an opponent and then turn in so that your front wheel ran over their front wheel. If done correctly they stopped very suddenly and you could get ahead. I did this to Stephen Wilson and of course he was not prepared and fell quite badly and went home. Later there was a visit from his mother very upset that I had caused him to hurt himself. I never saw him again.

I used to very much look forward to Bonfire night. My mother made treacle toffee and parkin. Sometimes we put potatoes in the fire to bake. We used to cut off the charred skin to get to the potato. I remember one year having some bangers and jumping jacks and going out with them in my pocket to cause mischief.

I was caned twice at Barker Butts – once for getting a low mark in a religious knowledge test and once for flicking ink at a boy sitting in front of me. The caning was done on the hand and wow did it hurt. Blood blisters come up on the palm and fingers.

My father had some kind of falling out at Bermetals where he worked in Coventry. He did have a bit of an attitude, that everyone else is an idiot, a trait of other family members. Of course, I have largely grown out of it. Someone came to the door after he had been sacked – a colleague I think – or maybe connected with the union. They had paid £1800 for the house in Coventry but, unfortunately, when they came to sell there was a bit of a mini recession and in the end they had to take less than they paid for it.

He then got a job with Britannia Iron and Steel works in Bedford, an old established firm that had been bought by a Swiss engineering company – George Fischer AG (GF) based in Schaffhausen, Switzerland. They concentrated on casting metal pipe fittings for things like central heating. He asked me for my ideas about the new house and I drew one that had a balcony. I don't know really where that came from but he poured scorn on it. I thought "what's the point of asking me, if you are going to rubbish what I say". He certainly commuted back and forth for quite a while and, as I say above, I think that was when he bought his first car. Interestingly his father had a car before the war, a Riley, with the story that it ran poorly and, when they investigated, the found one of the four cylinders had been blanked out. The car was a Standard and it required work. He had to get the engine out with a hoist in the garage and rebuild it. There were car parts all over the lounge floor for a while.

Just before we left Coventry my brother Martin arrived on 11th March 1957. My mother was up and about the day before, getting in the coal and minding the house. She had the baby at home.

Bedford 1958

We moved to 10 Greenacres, Putnoe, Bedford and I started at Goldington Road School. We had a new four-bedroom house on a new estate with an upstairs bathroom and toilet and another toilet downstairs. There was a large "L" shaped lounge and a kitchen with a coke-fired central heating boiler. It had quite a large garden and a detached garage with a flat roof and a covered alleyway in between. It took some time to get the garden sorted. My father laid a concrete path and put in a clothes pole for the washing line. He also started on a little patio area outside the back dining room area but never properly finished it. I had a go at digging over what was basically a field at the back but didn't get very far and eventually it had to be rotovated and lawns and borders laid. The front garden was lawn to the left of the path to the front door and a rose bed on the right. I think that they paid around £2500 for the house and funded it with a with profits insurance policy. These have since been discredited as investments, but my mother and father did very well out of it, even withdrawing funds before it matured.

I am not sure what his position was – foundry manager, engineering manager? He must have been put in charge of a modernisation programme because he went to Germany quite often in order to evaluate and buy new machinery for the foundry. The managers were Swiss and one of his colleagues was called Häberli. He must have overlapped with my father for a while before returning to Schaffhausen. Some years after we moved to Bedford, I remember them inviting us round for tea at their house. It was large GF-owned house on the embankment in Bedford. It was a bit of a disaster as we didn't like any of the food presented such as meat in aspic (jelly really) and some kind of cream dessert. They had a little girl and a boy called Thomas who beat up my brother Martin with a wooden hammer.

Goldington Road and Newnham Schools

I got on fine at Goldington Road School and made quite a few friends. However they opened a new school in Putnoe called Newnham Secondary Modern. It was much closer. About half of my class transferred, but I remained friends with three boys who stayed – Trevor Haylock, David Bayliss and another boy whose name I can't recall. We all four remained in touch until I left Newnham. However I was part of a new cohort, which progressed through the school as always the senior class because they started with just one year and added others progressively with new admissions. I remember some of the girls at Newnham, particularly Mollie Deacon and her friend Katherine Koblenz. The main friend I had was a boy called Jackson and also James Jowett and Goobie (I don't think we ever used his first name). Goobie's father owned a mini market like the Spars you see nowadays. Jackson still lives in Putnoe, as does Trevor Haylock.

Greenacres was on the edge of town at that time with a small shopping centre just to the north of us with a library and Methodist church. There were more shops down Queens Drive. Putnoe lane continued out of Bedford going past Putnoe woods and then eventually petering out into a track cum footpath that led to a village called Ravensden. The woods still exists and I loved going there in the summer. It is now part of Mowsbury Park, which was just fields at the time.

There was still a farm at Putnoe when we first moved and I was sent to buy eggs every so often. The farmer kept basset hounds and we used to hear them when he took them out in the fields.

Newnham was a good school for me and some of the teachers were very worthy of respect and others not so much. Mr Frank Richards taught English and other subjects including music appreciation. He also wrote and directed school plays. He had been at Goldington Road School. One incident there – he was doing some kind of lesson and a bit of a quiz and he asked the name of a famous English composer, giving some clues. As I say, I was reading very widely, and I realised that he was referring to Delius (1862–1934) but I was a bit too shy to put my hand up. When nobody answered and he told us the answer I said I had known the answer, to which I got a dismissive reply – "you should have put your hand up then shouldn't you" – and he probably did not believe me. Yet another lesson for life. His music lesson comprised of playing selected pieces to the class. I particularly remember him playing Ravel's *Bolero*, which stuck in my mind. He wrote pieces for the *Bedfordshire Times*, the local paper.

Mrs Willows was the geography teacher and I enjoyed her lessons. She was tall and willowy. Goobie tried to disrupt her class a number of times. He was quite a well-built boy. We must have been 14 or 15. She came across to him, said "Stand up", and then slapped him around the face with plenty of force. She said "Sit down" and he did. Goobie humiliated and lessons no longer disrupted.

Mr Monaco was the technical drawing teacher. Adjacent to that was the woodwork room – and that was another lesson I enjoyed. Science had been a bit problematical and we did have a useless teacher for a while. He impressed my parents though at a parents evening. In contrast he said to the class one day "what is the point of teaching you lot science subjects when the nearest you will get will be a hardware store". A newly qualified woman teacher then joined the staff. Her husband taught at Bedford School (the public school) and ours was the best position she was able to get. We were at the stage of deciding on which "O" level GCEs to take and she put me in for chemistry.

I must have just expressed an interest when we did lessons in the subject as part of a general science curriculum. My father had a number of chemistry textbooks, including one on inorganic chemistry that I had read. He had studied chemistry at some stage, whether as a subject in its own right or as part of other studies. I think that I was the only one to study chemistry and I must have gone in and had extra lessons. Anyway I passed the exam and then after that she moved to New Zealand with her husband. I regret that I do not remember her name. However, some years later, probably when I was at university studying chemistry, my father pointed out an article in the *Bedford Times* reporting that she had drowned in New Zealand. I shed a few tears. I have visited Bedford library twice to go through back issues of the paper to try and find the article without success. If she had not encouraged me to study chemistry then I would not have had any science "O" levels, would not probably have gone to the grammar school, would not have gone to university and obtained a B.Sc. and then a Ph.D.!

Several times, we went on summer holidays to Teignmouth in Devon. The first time I nearly died there. I had been given a pair of flippers and was swimming in the sea. It must have been a small cove because there were rocks and a cliff. The water was not deep but I got into difficulty because I was unable to get my feet underneath me because of the flippers catching in the sand. I was face down in the water and coughing and trying to get a breath and I had a clear vision that I had to get my feet underneath me and get my head above water or I would drown. With a major effort that included things going ping in my knees I managed it. My parents wondered why I wasn't that interested in the flippers after that, because I did not tell my parents what had happened. I also remember having a holiday in Colwyn Bay in North Wales but I am not sure when it was. We had a car because the engine boiled when we went over the horseshoe pass which is just off the A5 but heading to the coast from Llangollen. I had an exciting time playing on the beach, building sand castles and then having to retreat as the tide came in and starting over again.

The family acquired their first record player around this time. It was a "Bush" with a snazzy blue and grey case. We took the *Readers Digest*, which I enjoyed reading. It had an offer of a classical music selection. I think that there were 12 LP records in a case and it ranged from Tchaikovsky to Ravel with many pieces. I definitely played them all, but am not sure how much interest the rest of the family took. I purchased my first record – the Beatles' LP *Please Please Me*, which was released in March 1963. I purchased all their LPs after that. Later I became a bit of a Rolling Stones fan and bought a couple of their albums.

During one holiday in the summer I cycled from Bedford to Brockworth near Gloucester to visit my Aunty Edie and Uncle Bill. The day started fine and my mother told me to buy a fresh peach on the way if I saw one. Delicious! As the day progressed the weather deteriorated and I faced a head wind. I started at about 9 in the morning, maybe earlier, and I became more and more exhausted. At one point going up a hill in the Cotswolds I ground to a halt and just fell with my bike onto the grass verge. A car stopped to see if I was OK but I got up and kept going. I arrived after it had gone dark and they were surprised to see me as they thought that the weather would have put me off. Definitely character building as I had to keep going. After a rest day I rode to Monmouth across the border in Wales and back to Gloucester. I rode back to Bedford without incident.

I obtained English language, maths, geography, woodwork, and chemistry "O" levels but failed art, bible knowledge and geometric and mechanical drawing (1962). We had a trial exam the year before from the College of Preceptors and I got passes in English language, geography, physics, arithmetic, woodwork and technical drawing (June 1961). I was quite interested in painting at that time but found it difficult to get inspiration under pressure of an exam, so I failed it miserably. The teacher came round towards the end of the art exam and said that I had done more in the last 10 minutes than the whole of the previous two (?) hours. I have tried a number of times to start painting but never really had the time. My interest in design continued and in business later used it to produce what I thought were effective sales leaflets with the help of a proper artist!

At one point I had a period of getting to school late. The form teacher was Mr Richards and finally he gave me a severe warning. So the following day I got up early to make sure I was on time. However my mother told me to go to the chemist to pick up a prescription. Although I protested, she made me go and said I had enough time. She wasn't aware of the warnings I had had. Of course I was late again and when I tried to tell Mr Richards he blew his top and sent me to the headmaster - Mr Something-Small (yes, although I can't remember his whole double-barrelled name, it definitely ended "Small"). So I had to go and explain myself to him. I was upset and humiliated but he just sent me back to class and nothing more was said. I wasn't late anymore.

The school was not violent but there were occasional fights. There was an unpleasant boy called Booker who liked to provoke conflict. One day he challenged my friend Jackson to a fight after school. They duly squared up and I was on Jackson's side, but no one else got involved. Booker attacked Jackson who immediately got him in a head lock and shook him about until he gave in. End of fight.

The first girl I fell in love with was Jennifer Buckley Jones. My interest was hidden and she probably never noticed. One day at games we were playing rugby. There was an unpleasant Polish boy and as I went to tackle him in the usual way – grabbing him round the waist to pull him down – he elbowed me in the nose, blood everywhere. I was taken inside and, as it turned out, Jennifer was there and mopped me up and stopped my nose bleeding. Later the PE teacher took part in the game and gave the Polish boy a bit of a thump because he hadn't played by the rules. The PE teacher courted Jennifer and I heard that as soon as they were able they got married. Not something that is allowed nowadays!

My second crush was on Mollie Deacon. I remember at Goldington Road her sitting next to me in maths and noting what a short skirt she wore. Again I kept my feelings to myself.

Once, whilst at Newnham, as I cycled home I saw her ahead of me and decided to cycle next to her to chat. She told me to get on and overtake her!

After the "O" levels in the period before official school ended we were more or less let go. However I had been working in woodwork on a coffee table and I went in after school hours to finish it off. I still have it. I also had made a drawing board and set square that I was very proud of. It stayed in Bedford when I went to college and, on one trip back, I went to get it out of the loft. I was angered to find that drawing pins had been stuck into it by one of my brothers as part of doing some drawings, even though there were proper clips to hold paper.

A black boy joined our class in the fourth year. He was a West Indian called Reginald and he came to school in a very nice suit, whereas everybody else wore uniform. I befriended him a bit. He was a keen cricketer and, one day, bowling at me, the ball jumped from the uneven hard ground and hit me on the right cheek bone. Fortunately it didn't knock me out or my teeth and I think I must have moved to avoid it. I am sure it was not deliberate. Reginald developed mental problems and became withdrawn and eventually left the school. Many years later on a trip back to Bedford I ran into another boy called Taggart in a pub and he said that Reginald was still around in Bedford and still with problems.

My mother's father died during the time I was at Newnham and so Grandmother Bailey came to live with us. She was given a ground floor room that we used as study, as her bedroom. I don't think that she fitted into the family very well and eventually moved to Gloucester to stay with her other daughter Edie. I had a job delivering newspapers on a Sunday for which I got ten shillings, which was quite a lot. However the papers were very heavy and I had a special bike. The shop was in the centre of Bedford near John Bunyan's statue. The round was out around Putnoe and Brickhill and I had to walk up the hills until the load got lighter. I used the money to buy various things including an acoustic guitar for £12. The 60s were a time of change of course, but my Grandmother made some scathing remark about having money to burn "and what did he need that for". I set about trying to play it and learned a lot of the basic chords to accompany songs, but I never really had the time to dedicate to it. The guitar came to a sad end. I took it to college when I first went but, after the first year, left it at home and then it went into the loft. I went to get it sometime later and the bridge had become detached and the guitar was broken. I thought it was because of way the loft got very hot in the summer, but I have my doubts. My fishing rod also came to a sticky end when I went to get it from the loft one year. It had got itself broken. Not that I am accusing Martin, but he did like to take things to pieces.

My sister was very ill one winter. It had snowed and was very cold and she insisted on going out to play in the snow with the other kids. However she got a bad chest infection and was kept in her room for weeks. The house had a coke-fired central heating system so it got cold overnight as the coke burned out and it had to be relit most days. They were so concerned about Margaret that they got an electric convection heater and left in on permanently in her room. Eventually she recovered but ever after had a bit of a cough.

Stratton School 1962

So in the end I got five "O" levels – one of which was not academic. It was felt that I was worth educating further, and various options were discussed. In the end it was decided to send me to Stratton Technical Grammar School in Biggleswade, which was some way from Bedford. There was a bus there and back each day. It turned out that there were other pupils from Putnoe going in my year. The first day was pretty hard, turning from one of the top dogs, prefect etc. to dogsbody. This happens to everybody I suppose and going from Radford to Barkers Butts had been quite hard.

We of course stayed to lunch at Biggleswade (I had gone home from Newnham). At first I was stuck on the end of a table that had boys of various ages but with two older boys from the lower sixth (my form) and a fifth former at the top. The fifth former tried to humiliate me offering me "one chip or two" as they dished out the meals and passed them down the table. After a few days I got fed up and got there in time to sit at the top of the table. Of course when he arrived the fifth former was a bit irate and a scene ensured. A teacher was called but I kept my seat and, in the end, the teacher told him to get a seat somewhere else. There are always bullies throughout life and, for your own sake, you have to stand up to them. I palled up with some other boys (one of whom was my best man at my first wedding) and I moved to their table sitting at the top and dishing out the food! We had our own common room, which was on the first floor above the teacher's staff room. One of the games we played was to take someone's satchel and throw it out of the window. They would have to go outside and then crawl past the windows to retrieve their bags. The girls did not

seem to find these antics funny. In those days everybody got a
third of a pint bottle of milk, but a lot was left over. The bottles
were left in a corridor near an exit for collection. We used to
have milk-drinking competitions to see who could drink the
bottle quickest. I usually won because I had the knack of being
able to just open my throat and pour it in. I did not need to
keep swallowing. I suppose I could have put this to good use in
something really useful, such as beer-drinking competitions,
but I never did. Probably just as well.

My brother Andrew was born on 11th February 1962 whilst I
was at Stratton. There were three bedrooms at the front of the
house. Looking from the front there was a larger room for
Mum and Dad, and then Margaret's and then mine. There was
a larger room at the back for Martin and Andrew. Andrew
moved into my room when I went to college.

I stayed in touch with Trevor and friends. When I was sixteen
during the holidays between Newnham and Stratton we went
on a cycling holiday. There were four of us and our itinerary
was:

Lincoln, York, Ellingstring, Garsdale, Grange, Elterwater,
Coniston, Crossthwaite, Arnside, Barley (Pendle), Edale,
Bedford.

We stayed in youth hostels. Can you imagine cycling up the A1
to Lincoln nowadays? I was able to reconstruct this list after I
found the YHA map from this period and noticed that I had
circled all the above hostels. I have a photo of the four of us at
Aysgarth Falls in Wensleydale. After that I lost touch with them
all. Trevor left school at 16 and I am not sure what happened

to the others (although Trevor, it turned out much later, was still in touch with a couple of the boys)

Food

Time for another digression! I don't think that anyone born in the 60s or later appreciates how food has changed in the last 50 years. I ate exclusively at home with my mother's cooking until I went to Stratton school. They had lived through the war years with rationing, although for most people anyway the diet had not been varied in industrial Lancashire and the north. Potatoes were part of every dinner, with pasta or rice never putting in an appearance (apart from rice pudding). She did however make sure we had a range of vegetables, such as carrots, parsnips, cabbage, Brussel sprouts, leeks etc. Salads appeared only in the summer and were basically lettuce and tomatoes, sometimes with radishes and onion. Two things I hated as a child were cheese and tomatoes. Not just a dislike, I simply could not eat them. Of course a cheese salad was a terrible trial. We did not have a choice of meal – you ate what you got. Breakfast was toast and jam with bacon or eggs very occasionally. We had fish once a week and the meat was usually mincemeat with the occasional stewed beef. I remember liver turning up regularly, which I quite enjoyed. We had a turkey at Christmas as they got better off. Chicken only appeared on the menu much later, as did more expensive meats such as lamb or pork chops.

The meals at Stratton were pretty appalling by modern standards. There was no choice and dishes such as sausage pie appeared regularly – a flat pie in large tin trays with a thin layer of sausage meat covered with thick pastry. I can't remember ever having anything but chips with the meals there. In the summer salad was served – with chips of course. The chip pan also came out quite often at home. I remember one occasion when I think they still lived in Coventry when they must have been really hard up. The main meal billed as "Specials" was sliced potatoes dipped in batter and then deep fried. Delicious!

When we first lived in Bedford, as well as the local Putnoe shops, there was a Coop van that came round. My mum shopped with them every week. The family were much more prosperous in Bedford. Also my father was travelling to Germany and Switzerland regularly and got a taste for wine (he was never a beer drinker). My mother would buy a bottle of wine from the Coop van, usually German Riesling. He tended to stick with light white wines from then on, but my mother became more adventurous later. After one of his trips abroad my father was ill and was diagnosed with diverticulitis (an inflammation of the bowel). He was told to avoid vegetables from then on and, as he didn't really like them anyway, this was not a problem. Current medical advice is to eat more fibre for this condition – another example of wrong dietary advice based on minimum science. He never ate brown bread although my mother introduced us all to it. There have been a number of programmes on the TV about how we used to eat. On one of them there was a program on the war years. Apparently bread was restricted to the "National Loaf", which was kind of brown bread. However it seems to have had every bit of the wheat thrown in and may explain my father's distaste for brown bread. When I was around 16 or 17 they took us out for meals for the first time and we went a couple of times to a pub near Clapham. My father and I would have steak – Tornedos Rossini. You don't see it on the menu so often nowadays but it was a steak with pate and rich gravy on a crouton. The food culture in Switzerland had not been damaged by the war as much as the UK and he always enjoyed the food there.

I think that it was in Coventry that my father had his first Chinese meal while out for a business lunch. My mother had a go at doing one at home but I don't think they ever liked Chinese or Indian meals; hence I only discovered them when I went to college.

Stratton Again

I took "A" level maths, physics and chemistry at Stratton. As I only had four academic "O" levels I was advised to take another in order to reach the minimum for university entrance. They said that the easiest was biblical studies, so I did that for one year (and had studied it at "O" level). We did the Book of Kings (lots of sex and violence) and St Mark's testament. I also did additional maths at "O" level and then, at the time of the "A" level exams, we did an "O" level called the general paper, which I think covered a lot of subjects. So, I ended up with 7 "O" levels.

My mother and father were persuaded by a door-to-door salesman to buy a copy of the *Encyclopaedia Britannica* in order to help the children's general knowledge and education. It came with a nice bookcase with sliding glass doors. I think however that I was the only one who used it – I did enjoy dipping in at random to read about things and as interests occurred. I think that they felt that they had been a little bit conned by the military type with a moustache that had sold them it. After I left home, they sold it off but kept the bookcase. They also started buying the *Sunday Times* every week, which I devoured avidly. A colour supplement had just been launched and I remember that I cut out and stuck up copies of paintings by George Braque.

When I turned 17 I was taught to drive by my father in his old Standard 12. It must have been getting on by then and I remember that he had patched up the floor in the front where the metal had rusted through. The clutch had gone and so, to change gear, one had to "double-declutch", which involved taking the car out of gear (using the clutch) and then revving the engine to make the gears more nearly match up as you changed down. I failed my first test. I was on the way back to the test centre and I decided to overtake a cyclist coming up to some traffic lights. The lights changed, and I smartly pulled up in front of the cyclist causing him to brake. Failed! I passed at my second attempt. My mother was also taught at more or less the same time and of course she passed first time. After that my father bought a turquoise second-hand Ford Anglia. They had taken a look at a new small Vauxhall but decided the price and repayments would be too high.

I had a girlfriend at Stratton called Elizabeth Stankowska. She was also a sixth former and studied maths, chemistry and zoology. I was able to use the car to drive to Biggleswade and I took her to the pictures there a few times. We got as far as kissing and cuddling in the alleyway beside her house but I don't think her parents approved of me. I remember wandering around the school to find her during lunchtime. She was sitting on the grass with some girlfriends and I joined them. She made a remark about how wonderful it would be to be as free as a bird and I agreed. I later realised that this was a "get lost". She went to a teacher training college in the north or north-east somewhere when I went to London. We corresponded for a short while but that was that.

I don't remember being overly stressed by exams whilst at school. I kept up with the homework and read the textbooks. I am not sure I paid that much attention in class. In the final year my reading continued and I had moved onto the works of Dostoevsky – a Russian Victorian-era author and I do feel in retrospect that I was a bit depressed after reading his books and maybe that affected my exam results.

I applied for a university place to study chemistry and I went for interviews at a couple. I quite liked Leicester. Mum and Dad had bought me a new suit for my interviews. I remember it was dark grey and quite formal. I went by myself to Leicester and, after the interview, I had time for lunch before catching the train back direct to Bedford. So I went in a restaurant and had fish and chips. Actually it was an Indian restaurant!

That summer I went on a hitch-hiking trip with Adrian Savours and Peter Bilcock from Stratton. I had previously done a bit of hitch-hiking. I had travelled to see my Uncle Wilfred in Margate coming back via Portsmouth, where I stayed in the youth hostel. Wilfred was my mother's elder brother and he had married Edna shortly after the war. I have a cousin called Janet who was the same age as me but she had left home by then to start nursing training.

Wilfred had been an engineer before the war and then in the Royal Engineers. He had been in the army sent to France and had been evacuated from Dunkirk. He had stolen a bicycle during the retreat and, when he stopped for a quick drink on the way to the beach, came out to find the bike had been taken. He had to swim from the beach to a waiting ship in order to be evacuated. I don't know anything about his further war experiences. But after the war he and family moved back to Dukinfield and then they lived in Stockport. However Edna never liked the north and they moved to her home town of Margate. Initially, the only job he could get was as a milkman. He was really looked up to by my mother and Edie and I think that they regretted that, because of Edna, he didn't really keep in touch. My cousin Janet would be a better source for more information on him.

The trip we did was intended (by Bilcock) to be a bit of a "live off the land" type of journey to Scotland. We took a tent and a frying pan. We first stayed at a house in Edinburgh with a relative of Savours. One night we had been dropped off just north of Perth by a potato field. So we set up tent there, dug up some potatoes and fried them in the tent. Half raw potatoes with dirt – yum. We must have bought some food though. We got as far as Dalwhinnie on the way to Inverness and decided that we should venture no further north and took a westerly route south via Fort William. We had dreadful weather and pitched our tent by the side of a river just on the northern outskirts of Fort William. During the night the river flooded into our tent. I don't know what the others did, but I saw some lights on the other side of the road and went to take shelter and found myself in the local distillery, which was open, all lit up and lovely warm and dry. I was in the still room but didn't sample the product. The following day we walked into Fort William. I and Bilcock felt quite well, but tired. Savours was quite ill.

I managed to get away from them for a couple of hours and went into the station buffet and had a couple of meat pies. I don't think they had anything. Bilcock had been unable to forage for some food. We hitched in the open back of a lorry heading south but don't remember much about the journey to Bedford except for Savours chucking up at intervals. I wasn't much friends with Savours after that. He was a brilliant student with excellent "A" level results and I believe that after graduating from university in London he worked for ICL, the big UK computer company.

During that summer holiday I worked in the laboratory of GF in Bedford for 4 weeks. I did analysis of castings and materials.

I passed three "A" levels, but only at pass level "E". The university places I had been offered had required "A's" and "B's" so I wasn't able to get in. It was decided that I would go back to school in order to get better results. However somehow it came to our attention (I don't recall how) that there were a number of colleges in London that still had places and were accepting less good grades. I went for interviews at a couple and was accepted at the Northern Polytechnic in Holloway Road, London to study chemistry.

I had actually started back at Stratton when I got the news. The maths teacher was Polish. "It is your duty to study" he would say and when I told him while in his class that I was leaving to go to university he called me to the front of the class to congratulate me.

University 1964

Northern Polytechnic

It meant however that there was a bit of a rush to get ready to start a couple of weeks later in London. Schools went back at the beginning of September and colleges started at the end of September. There was a grant to sort, textbooks to buy, and lodgings to arrange. My grant was £330 pa with my parents being expected to provide £30 each year. It was a payable at the beginning of each term so I also needed a bank account. The college had quite a long history (founded 1896) and taught a range of academic and artistic studies. It also had a domestic science department. The chemistry department was well regarded and taught University of London internal degrees, which meant that the college was involved in the curriculum and setting examinations.

We had Thursday afternoons off for sports; otherwise it was 9 till 5 every day. I ate most of my meals at the college, either in the canteen or later in a café at the base of the new multi-storey science lab block (it opened in the second year). Otherwise it was old-fashioned tiered lecture theatres and labs with gas taps and benches.

My first lodgings were in Bounds Green quite a way out but on the Piccadilly underground line, as was Holloway Road. I shared a room with another boy. All my stuff was put into a large trunk and my father arranged for it to be delivered to my digs. However in a matter of weeks the landlady died and I had to get new lodgings. These were in Crouch End, which was nearer to college, but not as convenient as it did not have a tube station. I had my own room and there was another student studying medicine that I became friends with. The couple who owned the house were brother and sister and they had a horrible dog with lumps on it. They used to let the dog lick the plates after meals, which I thought thoroughly disgusting, and I am not sure how well they were washed afterwards. In the sitting room there was a bookcase with large numbers of books of Egyptian hieroglyphics. I don't know why the books were there. Maybe the chap was a noted Egyptologist, but at the time I was not interested. I went with my friend Jim to a number of student parties. At one of them I started drinking beer and then moved onto wine. Suddenly the carpet of the room struck me hard in the face. I had no feeling of falling, just the floor rising, and I passed out. I woke up on the stairs outside the flat feeling very ill and needing to clean myself up. I banged on the door until they let me in again and got to the bathroom. I don't know how we got back to the digs. The next morning I had the most terrible hangover and the landlady was disgusted with me. I couldn't face the greasy roast lamb Sunday lunch that they had prepared and had to get out for some fresh air. I stayed there until the end of term but then went and shared a flat with Peter Bilcock from school and another student from Queen Mary College.

The flat was near Lea Bridge Road – from looking at Google Maps, I think the address was 14 Wattisfield Rd. It was on the first floor and we had a front room with a double and single bed (I was in the single) and a small kitchen and bathroom. The three of us didn't really get on that well unfortunately.

There were a couple of further hitch-hiking trips around this time. There was a university-wide hitch-hiking competition to see who could get farthest from London and back in 24 hours. I took part with a guy from my class at Northern Poly. We signed up at Senate House in Bloomsbury and all set off together. We were allowed to use the tube in London. We went north to Glasgow via the M1 (only open to Crick) and then the A6. You had to get proof of where you got to and a police station in Glasgow stamped a form for us in the middle of the night. We got back within the 24 hours but someone had got a bit further north so we didn't win. On another trip I hitch-hiked with Bilcock and the other flat mate to Cornwall. We spent one night in a railway carriage at Penzance station which was quite comfortable. We were woken in the night by the police doing a check. We walked the last bit to Land's End. We were lucky to get a van coming all the way back to London overnight. It went to the old Covent Garden Market, which was the old vegetable market, and we saw it in full swing at 5 am.

At that time I had come up with the idea of a group of us buying a van and then driving to Greece in our summer holiday. We clubbed together, about 5 or 6 of us from Stratton, all having gone to college in London. It included Bilcock and Terry Lander. Terry had gone to Kings College Dental School, south of the river and he was later the best man at my first wedding. The van was a discontinued police van and cost about £70. I was the custodian of the van and used it a bit to get around. I usually cycled to college because, although not far away, none of the transport links went directly west to Holloway Road.

We had some adventures with the van. For example, we drove to Brighton after some kind of rave at Chislehurst Caves in South London and then drove down to Brighton. We stayed up most of the night.

However I fell out with Bilcock. We went to kick a ball around at a field over Lea Bridge Road and, while we were there, he deliberately kicked the ball to hit me in the face. Later back in the room we shared I threw the ball at him as he was sitting on his bed and hit him in the face back. We nearly came to blows.

Sometime after that he said we should just take the van to France for a week, which would have been a total let down and we decided to sell the van. Another group bought it off us to do exactly what I had planned and I nearly asked to join them and regret not doing so. On one occasion I drove the van to Bedford for a visit and parked it outside the house on Greenacres. The police came round the next day to tell us that the van had to have a light on it if it was to be left in the street and although I did get a little light to fix on a window we ended putting it onto the drive. We left it in the street in London with no problems. We didn't get quite as much for it as we had paid and a couple of the boys complained that they had never seen the van never mind used it, and it had cost them money!

Next thing our landlord died and his widow went through the whole Jewish mourning with wailing and lots of visitors for a couple of weeks. We had to leave.

During the rest of that term I had some lodgings with a lady who lived near Arnos Grove tube station in a flat above a row of shops. She was a bit strange and when a man friend came to call she would send me to the door to tell him that she was not in. One night I went to a party (I think with Jim from Crouch End) and stayed out all night. When I got back she wanted to know where I had been and then showed me a copy of the morning paper with the page open at a report of a jewel robbery somewhere in London. Not me of course. I found her interest intrusive and didn't stay long.

The next place I lived was south of the river near the Oval cricket ground and just along from the Oval tube station. It was a flat above a hairdresser's, and had a bedroom with three beds squeezed in and a lounge at the front plus small kitchen and toilet. I shared it with Terry Lander and a Greek guy who was also doing dentistry with Terry. We had a party and tried to take the sofa down the stairs to leave in the hall to make more room in the lounge. Unfortunately the sofa got stuck in the stairway and we couldn't move it so all the guests had to crawl under the sofa when going upstairs in order to get into the flat. It was definitely a conversation piece.

There was one strange incident at that time. Terry and the Greek guy got talking at the pub at the end of the road with some older men and they invited us all go to a party at the weekend. The three of us met up with this guy and he said he would take us in his car. We set off with him driving south eventually getting into the countryside – quite a long drive from the Oval. We started to get concerned and he kept on saying "nearly there". The Greek guy said not to worry as he had brought a knife with him. We asked him to stop as we needed a pee and we then climbed over a gate and ran off across the fields. He didn't try and follow and we kept going across the fields until we hit another road. We set of along the road back to London (this must have been after midnight as we had gone out with him quite late on); there was no traffic about and then right in the distance we saw what looked like the same car speeding towards us. We jumped into a ditch and kept our heads down and they shot past. Eventually we managed to get a night bus back into London. What was going on? I often wondered. I did ask Terry much later and he only vaguely remembered the incident.

I did go out with a girl that I met at a party with Terry. She was a dental nurse at King's college. I dumped her after going out a few times. However, this caused grief for Terry as he had introduced us and his name was mud for a while amongst the trainee nurses.

The course at Northern Poly consisted of chemistry part 1 after two years, and part 2 at the end of the third year. There were compulsory courses in maths (one year), physics (two years) and scientific German (one year). So at the end of the first year we had to pass maths and German. It was not too hard although quite a few dropped out after one year. Academically the year went well and I passed the exams without difficulty. I did get the time wrong for the German exam, however, and turned up half an hour late. Luckily no one had left the room and they allowed me to sit the paper. You were allowed to use a scientific German dictionary whilst doing the exam and I had done a bit of German at night school at Newnham School whilst at Stratton. I did have bad dreams in later years about turning up late to exams and failing the whole course.

At college I was friends with a Chris Harris and a boy called Mark Kelly. They both lived at home, as did quite a lot of the students on the course, Chris in Welwyn Garden City and Mark just near Archway at the top end of Holloway Road. There was a girl that I liked in the class called Mary who had ambitions to be a ballet dancer but was doing chemistry to have an academic qualification to fall back on. There was only one other girl. I joined the college debating society and in my first debate was called on to speak in favour of a motion about the Beatles. I made the point that there would be a dispute many years from now over who had actually written the Beatles' songs (of course a joking reference to the authorship of Shakespeare's plays). Maybe they were all written by the Rolling Stones? At this time and into the next year I used to play bridge in the common room and got quite involved. There were always a few games going on even when you would expect everyone to be at lectures.

None of us had much money. I worked the night shift at the Post Office in Bedford each year at Christmas and came quite well out of it. I was busy at college all week plus coursework but I remember we went to a concert at the Albert Hall to hear Tchaikovsky's *1812*. We also went one New Year's Eve to Trafalgar Square but didn't get into the fountains! Terrible crush even then. We heard on the news that Winston Churchill was very ill and, at Bilcock's suggestion, we went to stand outside his London House in Kensington. He died the next day, 24th January 1965.

That summer break I got a job at Unilever's research laboratory in Sharnbrook near Bedford. There was a bus each day. It was pretty boring stuff and all I remember doing was analysing the SO_2 content of frozen peas. It was added to keep them green after freezing and reheating.

Because of the sale of the van, I was at a bit of a loose end for an actual holiday and I contacted my German pen friend Horst Worbs, who lived in Munich. My father had got the correspondence started on the basis of swapping stamps. Horst bought me German issues as they came out and I did the same for him with UK stamps. He had visited Bedford by bike during the summer a few years before and had stayed with us. We had cycled to Cambridge (which I also did a few times with Trevor and Co). We hired a punt on the river. His English was quite good. He told me something that had puzzled him whilst on the way. He had gone into a café in London, read the menu and saw "Hot Snacks one shilling" and of course had ordered a "Hot Snack" the café owner was a bit baffled and was unable to serve him. I explained that it meant that there were a number of hot snacks available but you had to specify which one! He had never had a fried egg before, so was a bit baffled how to handle it when my mother cooked us bacon and eggs for breakfast. So I wrote to him to see if I could visit him.

I travelled from London with a special student train that I had booked through college. It eventually arrived at Munich East station where Horst met me. saying foreign trains didn't normally stop there. We spent a few days in Munich in an area called Schwabing near the centre where they had a cramped flat. We then went travelling to Austria by hitch-hiking although he was very worried that the police would stop him as it was forbidden in Germany. First we went to Berchtesgarden (15th September 1965) and then to Salzburg. I had obtained a German Youth Hostel card, which I still have, with stamps showing where we went. We then returned to Munich for a few days. I remember particularly enjoying German beer for the first time. We didn't have much money (I took £30 for the whole fortnight) and if we ate at a restaurant it was usually sausages and kartoffel salat – bratwurst or weiswurst, both of which I actually quite liked, with potato salad. We also bought shaslik from street vendors. It is a barbecued lamb dish like a kebab with a hot sauce coating and I think got to Germany from Turkey.

We then went travelling again and planned to go up Zugspitze, the highest mountain in Germany. We went south by train to Garmisch-Partenkirchen and set off from there. I had not done any serious hiking before. An experienced walking friend of Horst joined us and we made good progress. However about midday, a party coming down stopped to warn us that it was snowing higher up the mountain. We continued and it did start snowing. It got so bad that we were finding it difficult. I had taken my rucksack with all my stuff in and the other guy took it to help me and was surprised at how heavy it was. We struggled on until we found a mountain hut to stay the night in. I remember hearing rats running around in the walls of the place. It was near a cable car station and the following morning we took it down to Innsbruck in Austria. We stayed one night in Innsbruck in the youth hostel (21st September 1965) and then travelled to another mountain hut on the other side of the valley called the Weidener Hutte. I don't recall the return journey to Munich or the train back to the UK. This Alpine adventure did stick in my mind however and much later after I had retired I went for a week's hutting holiday with Ramblers Holidays in the area north of Innsbruck.

I had now decided to get my own place rather than share and managed to get a bed sit back in Crouch End. I liked the area and the nearby Muswell Hill. The course was uneventful but quite intense. I went out for a while with a girl called Sue Ellis who was studying maths and chemistry. She was not on my chemistry course and maybe she was a year ahead of me. She certainly was a bit more mature! We went to see a film called *The Collector* in a theatre near Leicester Square but she didn't like it. The film starred Terence Stamp as an oddball who inherits some money and then kidnaps an art student. Cue mayhem when she tries to escape and they have a fight in the rain involving a shovel. The film ends with her dying and the man looking for someone else; perhaps, he had aimed too high – so he stalks a nurse … So films involving attacks on women are not new (ref scandi noir films and books in the 2010s).

One night I arranged to go with Mary and her flatmate Jenny Stephens and another boy, whose name I cannot recall, to a folk evening at a pub in the area. The girls lived near Tufnell Park tube station and, although I say flat, it was just a shared large ground floor room in an old house. At the end of the evening he got friendly with Mary and I got friendly with Jenny – so that is how I met my first wife. She was also a student at Northern Polytechnic but a year behind me doing a degree in botany and zoology.

We would meet up most evenings and study in the library before going back each to our lodgings. I used to play badminton at this time in the college gym and together we started doing judo in the same class. We each got the special jacket and trousers and I suppose progressed quite well. I learnt to fall and also was able to do a forward-rolling somersault and land safely. I also did trampoline but gave it up after falling off a couple of times. Jenny and I eventually started spending weekends together in my bedsit. We decided we wanted to get married and I took her home to meet my parents.

At this point I should mention that I much later found Jenny's diaries and published them in 2008. (*Sail on Silvergirl*, Ultimate Publishers UK, ISBN 978-0-9558562-0-4). I have decided to write a separate account here of my life during this period rather than putting in my comments from that book. The book includes background on her family and life before I met her.

The weekend in Bedford went reasonably well, but my parents insisted that I finish my degree before we got married. Her father insisted that I should be confirmed and, to keep him happy, I was confirmed at Christ Church on Crouch End Hill. I had been previously confirmed as a child but didn't realise!

At Easter that year we decided to have a weekend away on the south coast. We hitch-hiked to Hythe and then down the coast until we found a B&B. It was just behind some sand dunes right on the coast. We had wonderful weather and sunbathed and I played on the sands as I had done in Colwyn Bay. In the evening we walked a bit further down the coast and found a pub to have mushroom soup and steaks. A golden moment and days to always remember!

The part 1 exams were at the end of that term and, although separate results were not published, I was sure I did well. I put it down to all the time we had spent in the library studying together in the evenings. The part 1 counted quite considerably to the final exam results.

That summer my father got me a job at George Fischer AG in Schaffhausen, Switzerland. I worked in a modern office type building, in the chemistry laboratory. I went out by train and had lodgings with a couple called Bauman in Flora Weg. The factory and laboratory was down in a gorge – Mullertal – and, although it was very close, it involved walking down many steps. The breakfast was fresh baked bread, butter and jam with freshly brewed coffee. I really enjoyed the breakfasts and must have eaten half a loaf sometimes.

My mother had always liked real coffee, and this was at a time when instant was completely ubiquitous. There was a coffee roasting shop in Harper Street, Bedford just opposite Marks and Spencer's (now closed) where you could select the beans (already roasted on the premises of course) and have them ground. At first she used a jug to brew the coffee but then they got a percolator.

I ate in the canteen and there were a few other summer students. It was the first time that I tried pasta (apart from Heinz spaghetti) and gnocchi. They served it instead of potatoes quite often.

One day the director of the laboratory asked me to go to his office. He gave me a task of totalling up columns of numbers using a mechanical calculator. When I gave him the results he blew his top and started shouting at me. I had been taught to put a single downward stroke for a 1 and for a 7 to have the top bar. This was pretty clear to me and when at college in England. The Swiss always put a bar across the 7 to distinguish from a 1, which was written with an upward stroke at the top. He said he couldn't use the results and would not listen when I started to explain how we did it in England. He didn't give me any other tasks.

Jenny joined me for my final two weeks of six and she lodged at another house on the other side of the Rhein also with a family called Bauman. We would meet up in the evenings and weekends. We did trips to the Rheinfalls by tram and also went on a river cruise to Stein am Rhein, a picturesque little river town. The Häberlis had bought a house in Putnoe (before finally going back to Switzerland) and I used to babysit for them. They would leave me a bottle of wine to finish whilst I was out (usually Beaune). The Häberlis invited us round for a meal one evening in Schaffhausen. On arrival she asked us was there anything that we didn't like. Jenny said anything but sausage. Cue awkward silence. Well it wasn't quite a sausage as it turned out, being a large pink thing that was cut into slices. I knew we had outstayed our welcome when he started massaging his chest and looking suggestively at his wife.

At the end of my job we set off to explore Europe a bit travelling by, of course, hitch-hiking. The plan was to visit Lake Maggiore because my father had been there whilst working in Schaffhausen and recommended it. GF may even have had a holiday place for staff. Our itinerary was Schaffhausen, Zug, Gotthard Tunnel, Airolo, Locarno, Feriola (both on the lake). We then decided to cross the Alps back to the Rhone Valley via the Simplon pass. We stayed in Visp and then travelled to Zermatt. We stayed another night in Visp. A mad decision was then made that we should go to the south of France and travel back to England from there. Mostly we stayed in youth hostels to keep the costs right down. In Airolo we stayed in a little guest house run by an old lady. She brought us breakfast in bed that morning – toasted baguette type bread cut thin across the loaf with butter, jam and coffee. Our route was across the St Bernard pass to Aosta in Italy. Our next stay was the YH in Cuneo south of Turin. We went out in the evening and in the square some men had a live turtle. Jenny was quite upset that they should be manhandling it. Then on to Nice and a bit of sunbathing on the beach.

This is where things started to go a bit wrong. The trouble was that the French were not that into giving lifts and it took a few days to get to Avignon. We had expected to get to Paris in a day or two but at the rate we were travelling we realised that we were going to run out of money before we got there. We decided to take the train to Paris and arrived there with just enough for the youth hostel. Jenny had some money available in a UK account. She tried to arrange to transfer it to Paris. Bank Holiday! We went without food for a day but the money eventually turned up and we got a train to London. Then she went to Wimbledon and I to Bedford.

Final Undergraduate Year 1966

For my final year and Jenny's second year we decided to try and get some kind of joint lodgings. In the end we shared with Mary and got a top floor flat in a house in Hornchurch, a short bus journey to Turnpike Lane tube on the Piccadilly line. The landlady and her son lived on the ground floor, the next floor had a shared kitchen and a couple of bedrooms and we had two rooms on the top floor under the eaves. Jenny and Mary shared a larger room and I had a small room. The landlady, Mrs Hosier, was definitely mad, and would shout up the stairs at us. Her son hovered around and would apologise for her.

That first term some students on the floor below us got so cold one night that they took the curtains down and used them as bed covers. Cue more screaming and shouting. The whole house used to shake whenever a bus went past! The poor digs made for quite a horrible year all round. It was tragic in view of what later occurred to Jenny. We had not been able to be together properly. Anyway we survived. The exams did not go quite as well as the year before and I got a lower second class honours degree. We got married that summer in Wimbledon. My father lent us his car for our honeymoon and we drove from Bedford to Aberdovey in Wales and had a pleasant week by the seaside.

Ph.D. Research

Jenny also passed the exams but had a further year to do for her degree. I had fancied staying on at the Northern Poly to do a Ph.D. but was a bit unsure about whether they would consider my degree good enough. Anyway I was offered a research post and I did wonder if it had been helped by good results in my part 1 exams. I was interested in inorganic chemistry and was offered a place with Dr Malcolm Fraser's research group (he was head of department) or with a Dr Goldstein down in one of the spectroscopy laboratories. The suggested choice was low frequency spectra of metal halide complexes or of liquid crystals, which were a bit of a chemical oddity. Maybe I would have got in on the ground floor with the latter – especially as they have become big business with LCD displays as a major application. I put Dr Fraser's nose out a bit by choosing Goldstein. However, seeing later what the other students of Fraser researched, I realised I had made the right decision.

Fraser went on to be a Professor of Chemistry at East Anglia University and Goldstein became head of department at Sheffield Polytechnic (later Sheffield Hallam University) and then was Vice Chancellor of Coventry University.

So I started work on the low frequency infrared spectroscopy of metal halide compounds. Ordinary infrared spectroscopy (IR) was already well established for the identification of organic molecules. Low frequency IR of inorganic molecules was being developed at that time. The frequencies of vibration were much lower because the atoms involved were much heavier or the vibrations were between groups of atoms. You will find descriptions of infrared (vibrational) spectroscopy on the Internet.

An instrument called an interferometer was used. The samples were pressed into polythene discs and then put into a vacuum chamber before being scanned by the interferometer. This was a more complicated way of obtaining a spectrum than an absorption spectrometer but had the advantage of scanning all frequencies at the same time. The problem was that a computer was needed to unravel the spectrum from the interferogram. So this led me into computing as well as research chemistry. I went on a course run by the college on the programming language Algol and was able to make minor changes to the programs. The interferometer produced punched tape and then this was taken to the computer centre for processing. Results came back as a series of numbers and a graph plotted on the output of a teletype. So I spent the next three years in the laboratory and also on teaching duty. I was employed by the college as a demonstrator and was paid a salary of £600 pa – a big jump from my £300 grant.

We got ourselves a small flat at 22 Tetherdown in Muswell Hill. The house was owned by a Mr Reginald Crane and he had a sign outside the door "Commissioner for Oaths". The house was three storeys and we had the top floor consisting of a large bedroom and siting room. We had a small kitchen and bathroom on the landing below. Mr Crane occupied the rest of the house with lounge downstairs, large kitchen and dining room and two or three bedrooms on the first floor. He must have been in his seventies or eighties and had never married.

He had a sister who came around every so often to bully him and give the place a clean-up.

So Jenny continued with her degree and I started my research work. We kept more or less the same hours travelling back and forth to the Poly. I remember one incident as we came home together from Highgate Underground station. We were walking through Highgate Woods and an old lady coming towards us said "May you go hand in hand in happiness all your lives" and we were very touched.

I bought my first car at a garage in Muswell Hill – a Ford Consul. It was grey and purple, four-door with a bench front seat and column steering. I later painted it a horrible green (I liked it at the time). We used it to go to college and also to go to Bedford and Wimbledon. There was a Sainsbury's just round the corner and also a cinema – both seem to be still going at time of writing (2018/19). Muswell Hill was quite close to Alexandra Palace where I had taken my final examinations. There was just a small electric fire for heating in the lounge so, in the winter, we had to wrap up properly. No heating in the bedroom, bathroom or kitchen. The house had been built with coal fires and never modernised. One night we had gone to the cinema and, as we came out, it had snowed – magical. When we got back to 22 Tetherdown we found that the snow had blown through the cracks in the windows and was lying on the window sills. I was becoming a more responsible person at this time and I took out a life insurance policy with profits for £1000 on my own life with Jenny as beneficiary. I also remember a visit from another salesman who worked for the Royal Order of Buffalos, which was some kind of mutual society but also offering life insurance.

There no exams for myself and I worked steadily away. The Ph.D. students had been given a small common room, which was near to our laboratory in the old part of the college. Goldstein had two a few other Ph.D. students. I remember Gek Tok from Singapore and Yuo Ahlijah from Ghana. Gek was Chinese and quite small, whereas Yuo was a great big black man. I also became friends with a Bob Mitchell who started doing his research the second year.

The chemistry department had a contract to analyse the milk at the Dairy Show held in Olympia every year. The demonstrators were roped in to collect samples and bring them back to the Poly. We analysed fat and solids contents. This was used to rate the performance of the cows. I had lunch at the show one day with Jenny visiting and at another table Dr Fraser and another lecturer were drinking gin and tonic. Their enjoyment was evident. I had tasted gin at home in Bedford after my parents had bought a little drinks cabinet. My mum liked it at the time as "gin and orange". I took a small swig and was really put off by the medicinal/chemical taste. Of course, later in life I discovered G&T and never looked back.

For our holiday that summer we went to Norfolk for a couple of weeks. Not as adventurous as previous holidays.

Jenny finished her degree and started looking for work. She got a job at Davies' tutorial college near to Waterloo Station. It is still going under the name of DLD College. It helped students get extra "A" levels in order to get the place they wanted at university or medical school. Jenny enjoyed working there but found it much harder than at college. The hours were longer (with preparation and marking) and it was more intense. She started to feel under the weather and visited the doctor a few times. When she was a small child she had lived in Africa, in the Cameroons, where her father had overseen a plantation. She had come back with several complaints including something called filaria. They had been cured as a child. When the doctors found they were making no progress with her illness she was referred to the Hospital for Tropical Medicine in London.

Life Changes

I received a call at work from there from a very upset Jenny. They had been carrying out blood tests and, whilst sitting in the consultant's office, he had been called away. She looked at her file on his desk and noticed a comment in the margin "leukaemia?" I went there and found her wandering outside. She had run out of the building. The rest is unclear but I think that we must have gone back in to be told that further tests would be needed, but it seemed like leukaemia. She was admitted to St Bart's Hospital in London. The outcome was confirmation of a diagnosis of chronic myeloid leukaemia with a prognosis of two years. Apparently some patients survived for much longer. Of course we were totally devastated. There was no particular treatment and she was advised to lead a normal life for as long as she could. Nowadays I think the condition is largely treatable. Jenny continued at Davies' but found it harder and harder and eventually left. It didn't seem likely she would work again. She started to find life in our flat a bit hard as she had nothing much to do having been so active before. My parents suggested that we moved to Bedford to live with them whilst I completed my Ph.D.

We were very sorry to leave our flat and the carefree independent life we had led in London. We also sold the car which was a bit of a mistake because it would probably have lasted quite a lot longer. I commuted daily from Bedford to St Pancras and caught the tube to Holloway Road. Dr Goldstein encouraged me to start on my thesis around this time even though I had quite a lot further to go. However it was the right thing to do. I wrote up the background to the study and work so far and, in doing so, I realised that there was further work needed to test out our various hypothesis about the relationship between spectra and structure. I got more into the physics of vibrational spectra and so-called "selection rules". There was an alternative technique available called Raman Spectroscopy which resulted in vibrational spectra that arose by different selection rules. The rules were determined by the structure of the molecule and increased the diagnostic power of the techniques when used together. This involved taking samples of the molecules I had synthesised to Imperial College where they had a LASER Raman spectrometer I could use.

So I had a productive time during this period. Jenny settled into life in Bedford and was generally quite happy. At one point, feeling a bit better, she got a job at Bedford School for Girls to teach biology but quickly found it was too much for her. My three years at college were coming to an end and I was working on the final version of my thesis. This was typed up by one of the college secretaries using carbons to produce multiple copies. I submitted my thesis in August 1970.

First Job, First Own Home 1970

It was now time to think about work and initially I was
interested in a junior lectureship in a university chemistry
department. However, such appointments were thin on the
ground and we were in no position to try and get a post-
doctoral position abroad, which quite a few people did at that
time. So I started applying for jobs in industry. I had interviews
with Shell in Abingdon, and a handful of other places.
However, a contact of Dr Goldstein's from Leicester University
got in touch. He had been acting as an unofficial agent for a
French company called Coderg, which had developed a
powerful LASER Raman Spectrometer. He suggested that I try
and become their agent but working with him. I went for an
interview in Paris (my first flight). The interview was a bit
hurried and disorganised and I was only there an hour and on
the next flight back. I waited for many anxious weeks for some
kind of reply but it never came. Next thing Coderg did a
distribution deal with an old established UK scientific
instrument company called Hilger and Watts. Because I had
been to see them, Coderg suggested that Hilgers interview me.
I went down to London for an interview at their Camden Town
office and was offered a job at a salary of £1200 pa. There was
a bit of discussion regarding this salary but it was the going
rate for a new Ph.D. It was agreed to review my salary after 6
months. When that time had passed, I went to see the sales
manager. His response was to say that he would have to be
careful in future what he said to me! I joined the team at
Camden Town doing the marketing support for spectrometers
with a specialisation in the Coderg product. Hilger and Watts
produced a range of other spectrometers including infrared
(but not the far IR I had used for my research). The team dealt

with technical queries from the field sales team and produced all the quotations.

Once I had a job we decided to try and get our own house. We both wanted to live as normal a life as we could. Although I started out commuting from Bedford, the timing of the trains made getting to the office for 9 very difficult unless I caught a much earlier train. This was not a problem going into college because I could choose my own hours except when demonstrating. At that time there was a fast train from Bedford every hour, which came from Sheffield, or there was a more frequent but slower train that stopped at all the small commuter stations into London. We looked north of London but the prices were too high until you got out to Luton. We bought a small semi-detached house, 6 Nethercott Close, Luton. It was on the side of the town near the airport and I caught a bus at first to Luton station.

Jenny researched alternative therapies to treat leukaemia but didn't find anything that sounded any use. I believe that she had a relative who was still alive seven years after diagnosis. Some other relatives who lived in Scotland (I can't now recall how they were related or what they were called) gave us the money to buy a car. We bought a Ford Anglia for a few hundred pounds.

We moved house and got furniture, washing machine etc. There was only one piece of furniture we had from Tetherdown and that was an easy chair we had bought from Heal's in Tottenham Court Road, London which I still have. Her mother came to stay with us for a few days to help her settle in. Jenny had always kept animals, such as guinea pigs, when a child and we decided to get her a dog to keep her company. I don't know where she got the dog from but it came as a puppy. She called it Sheba. It settled in but was a bit strong willed and a handful.

Whilst with Hilger I got involved with exhibitions and sales conferences. I went to a Raman Spectroscopy conference at Oxford University and also a sales conference in Banbury. In both cases I stayed away to participate and felt guilty about leaving Jenny at home, although I think her mother came to stay.

That October/November there was the changeover to natural gas in the area so unfortunately the house was without heating for a week. One day at the end of November I persuaded Jenny to go for a little walk around the block but, when we got back, her legs swelled up and she felt quite ill. I phoned for an ambulance and she was taken to Luton and Dunstable Hospital. They decided straight away that the problem was the leukaemia and she was transferred to University College Hospital in London. That day I took Sheba to Bedford to stay with my parents.

I continued working but visited her every evening. The hospital is quite close to St Pancras station from which I caught my train to Luton and used the car to get home. I got into a routine and would have a meal after seeing her. I ate at an Indian restaurant in Grafton Street just over Tottenham Court Road. One evening I got back and found that the hose to empty the washing machine had become disconnected and the kitchen was flooded. I usually went to Bedford on Saturday and would visit her on Sunday evening. We hoped she would be able to come home for Christmas but it came and went. Her condition did not improve and in January the surgeon suggested that her spleen should be removed.

The operation took place at the beginning of February and she never really recovered, having a drain in her tummy till the end. Looking back, I doubt if it was worthwhile because she suffered dreadfully from having the operation. People tend to ask more questions of doctors nowadays – what impact were they expecting the operation to have on her life expectancy anyway? Her notes indicated that she expected the worst from this operation.

We tried to look forward and I brought in a selection of holiday brochures after Christmas. She tried to perk up at that time and I think the nurses made a special effort with her. However, she continued to decline.

I had gone to the cinema one Saturday night with Martin, my brother, to see *Lawrence of Arabia*. Whilst the film was on, a slide appeared on the screen asking Mr Unsworth to go the foyer. I phoned home and was told that the hospital had phoned and suggested that I go down immediately because Jenny had taken a turn for the worse. I drove down and parked the car in Grafton Way directly next to the hospital on a double yellow line. Jenny was in a side room unconscious with an oxygen mask on. She never regained consciousness. I stayed with her (except for overnight when they arranged for me to have a bed in the modern part of the hospital). She progressively got worse with a film on her teeth and lips and fungus on her ears and her breathing deteriorated. Her mother spent part of the time with me and I was able to go out to eat. Eventually on 25th February at 5 o'clock she died. She took a deep breath and then just stopped breathing. I said goodbye and called the nurse and felt quite literally a weight lift from my shoulders. I called home and my mother came down by train to take me home. My car was still outside on the yellow line, untouched and without a parking ticket and I drove us back to Bedford. It only got as far as Edgeware Road before packing up and it had to be towed to a local garage for repairs.

When I came to go through my trunk (many years later) and found her diaries, there was a set of ten notelets that Jenny had written after that Christmas thanking people for presents but that she had not posted.

A death like this makes one suddenly realise how many assumptions we make about life – having children, even grandchildren, careers, holidays, being with one person for the rest of your life. It is a shock to find how many of these things are fragile, and you realise that other things are going to happen in life that you can do absolutely nothing about. My mother surprised me some time much later (early 1990s) by stating that she had never worried about me because I had always bounced back! All I can say is well maybe – but I am sure life will hold further shocks.

Moving on 1971

I took a fortnight off work. I spent a few days in Bedford and then booked a skiing holiday to get completely away. Skiing had been on Jenny and my list of things we wanted to try. The flight went from Luton to Innsbruck and then we transferred to the hotel in Mayrhofen. I didn't have the meal provided, which was a bit of a mistake as I felt quite ill by the end of the flight. My hotel was just a short walk from the centre of the village and the skiing group met up at one of the central hotels. We were a mixed bunch of beginners from all over the UK. After our briefing I got talking to a girl called Margaret. and we went downstairs with some others to the Stubli or little bar.

The following morning, we collected our skis etc. and went up in the cable car to the nursery slopes. It was very sunny and we ended taking off our coats. After a few days of practice we were set loose on the nursery slopes. The instructor was a character and chased the girls quite a bit, telling them to go back to their rooms, take a hot bath and wait for him. We were taught snow plough turns, parallel turns and how to go uphill. It was very hard on the thighs and knees. The group more or less stuck together although we were in a number of different hotels. On one occasion we were in a cable car talking and I must have said I had chosen the holiday after my wife had died, someone else said she had gotten away after the death of her son, then another lady said she had just got divorced. There was an Australian there (part of our group) and, as all this came out, I could see him looking more and more disturbed and alarmed. What a bunch of unhappy people he was with. Margaret was recently divorced. Her husband had gone off with her best friend. She had been a nurse in Coventry but had moved back to Yorkshire as a health visitor based in Pocklington, just south of York. Her parents lived in Bridlington not far away. Since then I have always liked nurses!

On the last day, we set off down one of the easiest runs to Mayrhofen. I managed to get down but was extremely exhausted. The week included a fondue evening with each of us cooking meat in hot oil. It was a terrible fire hazard. Everybody was drinking and, at one point, standing on the benches to sing until the waitresses pulled them down.

I had intended to get contact details for a few of the people on the holiday but when we went through customs at Luton everybody just dispersed very quickly. My father was there to pick me up and take me to Bedford. As we drove in the car he said that Jenny's mother, Cynthia, had been to sort through all her things. I was very upset at this as I had not been asked and would have done so myself in my own time. I knew, however, that she had done it purely to get her hands on Jenny's jewellery, most of which had been given to Jenny by her grandmother. She had also taken Jenny's wedding and engagement rings, which I would have surely kept. I would have given them their family jewellery. What a miserable pair of parents. They were as described as such in Jenny's own diary and account of her early life.

I had, however, got Margaret's details and wrote to her when I got back and we kept in touch.

I went back to work in Camden Town and became friendly with one of the other trainees called Nigel Weselby. He was in the export department and mainly dealt with the overseas subsidiaries of Hilger and Watts. We also had some trainees working with us for a while from the Vienna office, which dealt with eastern Europe. I went out with the field salesmen to learn about sales and to back them up with the technical side that I specialised in.

Hilger and Watts was a much shrunken company. It was formed in 1948 by the merger of the two companies, both of which originated in the 19th century. It had done well after the war. However it was struggling when I joined. They had factories in Essex and in Margate in Kent. It had a very wide product range from large industrial analytical machines (e.g. GF had such an instrument in Schaffhausen to analyse steel from the furnaces) to small instruments for research laboratories. It also had little operations making specialised gas mixtures and a unit growing single crystals of things such as sodium chloride (which had been used in infrared spectrometers in the years just prior and had been replaced by diffraction gratings almost completely). I did wonder why they never got into growing single crystals of silicon (still the main component of computer chips) as the method was the same. However I think the management was poor and they were dividing their efforts over too many fields and not getting into a strong position in any of them. I think I was seen as a bit of an academic, too ready to voice an opinion, but they put up with me.

It was very difficult living in Luton by myself and I quickly resolved to sell the house and move to London. It had a buyer as soon as the estate agent listed it and the sale went through very quickly. Dr Goldstein had suggested that I should keep it but the market for rentals was poor and I didn't want the hassle. However it was a period of house price inflation and I lost out. I was disappointed to just about get back our deposit even though the mortgage had been paid for about six months. The car came up for its MOT and of course failed. I took it back to the garage in Luton and they reluctantly fixed it up to pass. I then traded it in and added the deposit money to get a red Mini 1000, which I really enjoyed driving.

Bedsit and Flat Share

I moved to a bedsit just off the Archway near to Highgate tube station. I stored some of the stuff we had bought and some was sold to the new house buyers, but I took a bed and my desk with me. It was an old large solicitor's type desk that we had bought at auction in Bedford at the sales yards. In the bedsit I had a kettle and a hot ring. There was a shared toilet. In the hallway there was a phone that the lodgers could use with a coin meter. One night, quite late, I heard a young woman on the phone in the hall outside my room talking very loudly to someone. She was slagging off her ex-husband who had reduced her to living in this grotty bedsit etc. etc. I got fed up and opened my door and said to her "Would you like a cup of coffee while you are on the phone". Of course I got a load of abuse and she slammed the phone down. When I told Nigel he thought it was very funny.

Margaret came to stay with me in my bedsit and I visited her in Pocklington. She took me to the theatre in York and I also remember us going to the cinema to see *Cromwell* with Richard Harris. She also took me out with a rambling group onto the York Moors even though I didn't have suitable shoes (no boots then). Fortunately it was dry and the only difficult part was over heather moors where the heather had been burnt off and the roots and branches caught your feet. The day finished with a ham and egg supper at a pub on the moors. This was my first introduction to hill walking and the Ramblers.

Nigel and his girlfriend Maureen had a ground floor flat in Cricklewood and invited me to join them. I had a small front bedroom and they had a larger front bedroom. There was also a large lounge with French doors to the garden, a large kitchen with dining table and separate bathroom and toilet. By coincidence Maureen also worked at Davies' tutorial college but she had never met Jenny. They were both language graduates from Swansea University. He was from Nottinghamshire and she was from Essex.

I decided to see if I could embark on an academic career again. For my summer holidays I took my mini to Germany and visited a number of universities to see if they had any research posts in my particular field. I particularly remember Marburg where there was also already an English post doc who I went to lunch with after meeting the professor. The mini was a great little city car but very tiring driving hundreds of miles on the autobahn. The trip came to nothing and I continued working in Camden Town.

I must have seemed different when I returned. I had spent two week more or less by myself. Nigel and Maureen had decided to get married and a date was set. I was surprised not to get an invitation. Anyway, I went to John Lewis and bought them a nice set of towels. They were touched by this and invited me to the wedding in Southend. The night before the wedding Nigel was ill with nerves so I took Maureen out for a Chinese meal instead of him. The wedding was in a registry office and, as we waited, Nigel looked worse and worse and said he couldn't do it. They decided to put the wedding off and Nigel went out to get some fresh air and calm down. The reception was all arranged so that went ahead without him. Eventually they got married later that day.

At this time I had kept my links with Goldstein and the Northern Polytechnic and I gave a short course for post docs on symmetry and group theory as it applied to spectroscopy and crystallography.

I was involved with the marketing for an infrared spectrometer – H1200 Infragraph– that Hilger had introduced a few years before. It had been successful particularly in the USA as a relatively cheap introductory level instrument. They decided to develop a higher performance model – H1400. It was also to replace a very old model that still used a NaCl prism. The timescale kept slipping and I am afraid that I christened it the "Infralaugh". I mentioned this in a memo, which did not go down well.

Hilger sent their sales manager to China every year to negotiate a large contract. Prices were inflated and most of the things ordered were already obsolete but kept in production for the Chinese market. The H1400 was never launched. I drew a couple of lessons from all this – the difficulty of introducing new products that make your old products obsolete and that R&D effort wasted is never recoverable. If the product is not developed in a timely way then the original premise for its development will likely be obsolete as will the product when it finally hits the market.

Hilger and Watts decided to close the office in Camden Town and relocate all functions to Margate. We were all taken for a day out to take a look at the factory and town. I decided it would be a dead end for me and started looking for another job.

I did have discussions direct with Coderg again regarding being their representative in the UK but it came to nothing. As you can gather from this, I had been interested in running my own business from early on in my career.

Varian Associates 1972

I started working for Varian Associates in Walton-on-Thames a few months later. I was employed as the UK salesman for a range of optical spectrometers made by a Varian company called Cary Instruments, from California. The target market was university and company research labs. They had been making a major effort with LASER Raman Spectrometers (LRS) and had two new instruments on the market. My salary went from £1200 to £1800 pa plus car. Of course at Hilger I had been the Raman product specialist for Coderg. I was very excited that I would be able to choose a new Ford Cortina – I wanted a bright yellow one. On my first day I found that they had already got me a white estate car! Going home back to Exeter Road in the dark after it had been raining and using the backstreets I skidded going round a corner and scratched the car. Gulp. I reported the damage next day. They were not pleased. My mini would have held the road with ease and would not have skidded.

My manager was called John Babb and, after I had had some product training from a Polish/French guy that they had sent over from Paris, he took me out for my first meeting to Harwell research labs. They were interested in buying a Cary 82 LRS. We had met at Harwell and he suggested I go cold calling at

Reading University on the way back to the office. So I knocked on doors and tried to find if anyone was in the market for spectrometers. I was pretty uncomfortable doing this but persevered.

I decided that getting to the office from Cricklewood was too far and looked for somewhere to live convenient for Walton-on-Thames. The M3 motorway was under construction so I based my search on that. I found that I had to go out as far as Basingstoke to find somewhere I could afford and eventually bought a flat – 12 Sylvia Close. It was modern with two bedrooms, kitchen, bathroom and lounge and had central heating from a common boiler. I had sold the house in Luton for about £3000, which was what we had paid for it. Prices had jumped up in the short period since and I had to pay about £7000 for the flat, which was a struggle. Of course I was able to sell my mini for the deposit. I got a mortgage and also took out a bank loan to cover things such as carpets. But it was very basically furnished.

I had stopped seeing Margaret some time before changing jobs. It had just stopped working. I had been contacted by Mary. I think she sent me a Christmas card asking me to get in touch and I started to see her. She was still a bit odd and had a job teaching chemistry at a college near Edgeware Road in London. She was doing ballet as often as she could. She lived in south west London, Turnham Green, I think. I took her out to the theatre and ballet. I invited her round the flat in Cricklewood one night when Nigel and Maureen had said they would be out.

I decided to make spaghetti Bolognese and we had a bottle of wine. The evening didn't go well. First she said that she hated spaghetti so I had to peel and cook some potatoes and then, just as we were getting comfortable on the sofa, Nigel and Maureen barged in. The last straw occurred on the day of the presentation of my Ph.D. certificate at Senate House, London with the Queen Mother presiding. I had invited my mother and father and Mary. We were to meet at Goodge Street tube station. We waited outside and Mary turned up a bit late with a bunch of flowers for my mother. She said she couldn't come to the ceremony and ran off. Maybe she thought that it wasn't time to meet my parents. I didn't see her much more after that.

Whilst at Hilger's, Nigel had a Chinese secretary and one night Nigel, Maureen and I went out for a meal with her and her boyfriend. We went back to their flat – somewhere off Holloway Road. They introduced us to his sister Mai. She was a trainee nurse at Whipps Cross Hospital. Later I asked if Mai would like to go to the cinema one evening and we went to the large cinema in Holloway Road. I have no idea what we saw. She had come from Ipo in Malaya. We gradually became quite good friends and used to meet and go for dim sum in Chinatown in London. However the relationship just petered out.

I then decided to try computer dating. This involved sending in a form with some money and then they sent you back a list of possible matches with phone numbers. I went out with a few girls but eventually clicked with a girl called Fiona who lived in Twickenham. This started whilst at Exeter Road and continued for quite a while after moving to Basingstoke. She would take the train down and stay the weekend with me. However after

a while she started to get on my nerves and in the end I
dumped her.

A New Life and Job 1972

I then joined a divorced/widowed club in Basingstoke and met my second wife Anne Vaillant. I was still strapped for cash and I moved into her council house in Basingstoke with her son and daughter, Stewart and Nicola, and rented out my flat. Anne came off benefits and was able to get a part-time job. Stewart's father became difficult when he found out that Anne had a partner. He used to wind up the little boy terribly. In the end, Anne decided that the situation was intolerable and she handed custody to the boy's father. They moved back to Africa and she did not see him again until he was in his thirties. Nicki settled down with no trouble and I adopted her. We moved back into my flat and lived there for a while. We got married that summer.

I found the salesman's job at Varian very hard for the first six months or so and even told my manager. He said it was up to me whether I wanted to continue. Things improved and I started getting business in after making quite a few mistakes. So I settled down and, after discussions with John Babb, I decided to take a course at Slough Polytechnic – Diploma in Management Studies. This involved a couple of evenings per week and was quite intensive as I was also working full time. The course covered lots of aspects of running a business – accounts, marketing, computers, managing personnel etc. We had a weekend away session somewhere in the area. One of the exercises was a simulated trade union dispute. I was a manager with colleagues and we were in negotiations with the union representatives. I must have got quite aggressive during the negotiations because in the round up and evaluation I was described as "Bomber Bill". I left the course at the end of the first year after I got the job with VG Isotopes. I looked at completing it at Keele University but I was really too committed at work. I had covered a lot of basic management stuff but it would have been advantageous to have completed the course.

I attended a Raman Spectroscopy conference in Rheims. Every day there seemed to be dinners and receptions including lots of champagne. Varian had sent over an American product specialist called Herb and I am afraid that we both missed one of the morning sessions.

I was sent to Warsaw to give a talk at a seminar on the Cary range of products. The night before, we were taken to the Palace of Culture for drinks and a meal. I drank quite a lot of "Bull's Blood" and felt terrible the next day but managed to give my talk. The girlfriend of the Varian rep who organised the seminar had joined us at the meal. On a later trip I saw her at one of the airport check-in desks. I said hello but she ignored me and pretended not to know me. I wondered what her real job was.

Because my territory was the whole of UK and Ireland I travelled all over the country mainly to visit universities. I tried to make my visits to places I had not been to and would take the chance to visit interesting places. I remember going to Stonehenge when the car park was just adjacent and there were no controls on accessing the stones or touching them.

It was during this time that I avoided death for a second time. I was driving to an appointment in Oxford and was running late. I saw a line of slow cars. The road in front of them was clear for some way. I decided to put my foot down and overtake but, as

I passed the first few cars, I realised that the car at the front of the queue was turning right. I was going much too fast and breaking would not have avoided a collision. So I put my foot right down, flashed my lights and leant on the horn. He saw me, braked and I shot past. Gulp. I am now a safe driver, honest.

Varian then decided to change the way the large expensive instruments were sold and, instead of covering the whole UK and Ireland for one product line, it was decided to create an area based sales team covering three product lines (Cary, NMR and Mass Spectrometry (MS)). I got the south of the UK. I went for product training to Bremen in Germany on the MS product line. I managed to get a large order (£100K +) for an MS from Glaxo Research in Greenford, which brought in a very nice bonus. I had already paid off my bank loan and we decided to move to a small house on the outskirts of Basingstoke. I made many trips to Varian MAT in Bremen with potential customers. They placed us in a hotel just across the river Weser from the centre of the city. We would go into the Schnoor district for meals and I distinctly remember the aroma as we came out of the hotel – Becks Beer and Jacobs coffee. The MAT factory was some way out of the town. MAT had been acquired by Varian just after Cary instruments. Varian had created an instrument group that also included gas chromatographs and atomic absorption spectrometers.

That summer I had to attend a training course organised by the European office of Varian. The conference was at a hotel in Morcote on Lake Lugano. Their office was actually in Zug in Switzerland and I also attended meetings there on a couple of occasions. I was able to take Anne and Niki with me by car. We borrowed a tent from Anne's father so that we could go camping after the conference. We loaded it on top of the car. Nikki was sick as we drove to catch the ferry. As usual I was probably driving too fast. We got across the channel OK and set off to drive to Switzerland. We were on the motorway at first and then onto a quiet ordinary road. Suddenly as we drove along I heard a loud noise and I pulled up sharply. The tent poles were scattered across the road. The bag they were in had split. I gathered all up again and secured, it thankful that it had not happened on a busy road.

I attended the conference each day and Anne and Nikki did what they wanted. An American woman was there with someone else from Varian and, amongst other things, they all went to an art gallery in Lugano itself. The hotel put on a barbecue one evening – the first I had set eyes on, but we couldn't attend because of the conference.

We then set off on our camping trip. We had booked into a little town called Kaprun in Austria. We stayed a couple of days but were disturbed by the cows in the same field especially when they were chomping away in the morning as we awoke. However the weather was cold and wet and we went over the Brenner Pass to Italy. We went to Lido de Jesolo at a campsite very near to the vaporetto station. We went to Venice a couple of times. It was much warmer than north of the Alps (Morcote had also been very warm and pleasant). One night there was a tremendous thunder storm but it was warm again the next day.

VG Isotopes Ltd and Up North! 1976

The next job move was prompted by a notice in the *Daily Telegraph*. Entrepreneurs in the instrument field were asked to come up with new business ideas. I got in touch with the product development manager from Hilger and Watts, who I had always got on well with. At that time Fourier Transform infrared spectrometers (FT IR) had started to be developed for the more common mid infrared spectrum (as against the far infrared that I had worked in for my Ph.D.). Partly it was the appearance of more powerful computers. I put together a business plan that actually started with the development of related instruments – monochromators - that were simpler and then moved onto FT IR. The company that had placed the ad was VG Instruments, a vacuum and mass spectrometry company based in East Grinstead and Winsford, Cheshire. The guy looking for ideas for them was a Robert Craig. We had a meeting but they didn't want to take it further. They thought that we should get straight into the FTIR field (which would have required both optical and computer expertise) and I don't think that they were too impressed with my fellow entrepreneurs.

The experience had however got me thinking about moving on jobwise and I was invited to an interview in Winsford for a management vacancy at VG Gas Analysis Ltd. The interview did not go that well. I applied for other jobs that came up in the instrument and related fields and for example had an interview with Oxford Instruments, makers of super conducting magnets.

The next Christmas I sent a card to Robert Craig and was invited back for another interview as marketing manager for a company called VG Isotopes Ltd that made isotope ratio mass spectrometers also based in Winsford. I got the job. The salary was £2500 pa and also included a company car. We bought a house in Hartford near Northwich and up north we went.

Initially I got lodgings in Delamere Forest, which was only a few miles from Winsford. The other guys staying there smoked, which made me feel ill. The factory was on the other side of Winsford. At the interview they had asked me for my opinion about the factory and offices. I had told them that it looked a bit run down and probably would not impress visitors. I was placed in an office with M. who was a director and responsible for the factory and technical support and services and a Garry Rowling. They both smoked cigars and the office was inside the building with no windows. Then they had the front part of the building redecorated.

I found it very hard going in that office. One of my first jobs as part of getting into the job was to issue a leaflet about an argon preparation system – basically a furnace to extract argon from rock samples so that they could be dated by a mass spectrometer. Craig (who was based in Altrincham with a bit of a roving brief having founded the MS business some years before) suggested that I speak to a graphic artist called Roy Partington who lived in Knutsford. The cooperation went well and I was to work with Roy on leaflets and adverts until he died suddenly many years, and a couple of businesses, later.

A visit had been arranged by the Italian agent for some scientists to discuss their requirements for an MS. I had expected to arrange the visit at our end, bringing in specialists etc. and generally making sure the visit went well. I would then have done the quotation. However M muscled in and took over the meeting. After the visitors had laid out their requirements he took to the blackboard and made a proposal for a special valve for the MS to allow gas sampling. Some weeks after the visit the agent contacted us to say that the order had gone to the competitor – Varian MAT – in Bremen, who I had of course worked for. An emergency visit to Italy was arranged for me and Ian Neale, the MD of the company, but it didn't change the customer's mind. Neale was very annoyed. He said that we should have offered the system that they had already spent years developing, not dreamt up something new. I told him how M had taken over the visit and the matter rested there. He must have said something to M because he tended to keep out of my hair most of the time after that. It was serious for me because I was new there and I had lost the first order that came up because the company had offered the wrong solution.

I tidied up the marketing operation. I put real effort into a customer mailing list, created and updated existing sales literature and revised the pricing policy. Previously they had a single price list no matter where the customer was located. 90% of the business was exports. I instituted a couple of different pricing levels and substantially increased prices for East Bloc and most other countries. This is what Hilger had done and it allowed for discounts to be given off the list if it was demanded. I created a sales agents book to allow easy reference by myself and directors to agents details, pricing etc.

I got another lesson in employee relations around that time. I had been playing squash at a place in Winsford with other employees. A couple of the engineers were moaning about salary reviews. This had been discussed at the weekly management meeting. I foolishly said that something was planned but didn't give any details. Next day I was called in by the MD to be told that it was all round the factory that management had agreed to offer a new deal on wages – according to Bill Unsworth. I was annoyed with myself, but had not worked in that kind of environment before, and with the engineer who had passed on my vague comment. After that I stopped playing squash with them.

We moved to 2 Massey Avenue, a four-bedroom house, in Hartford near Northwich. I had looked around at houses in Winsford, not really such a nice town, and also at Holmes Chapel and Sandbach. Hartford offered the best value and was convenient for Winsford and Manchester Airport. The house cost £14000. Nicky went to the local primary school just round the corner.

The first conference I went to was a Geochronology conference in Amsterdam, where we had a little stand. There was myself, the marketing director Geoff Overend and one of the senior engineers, Clive Haines. I was to give a paper on a new triple collector instrument for analysing isotopes of CO_2. We went there by car on the overnight ferry. The conference went well but I remember on the way back that our four-bunk cabin was joined by a drunken Englishman who caused consternation by falling out of his bunk in the middle of the night and cutting his head badly.

The management team was changed quite soon after I got there. Geoff Overend and Ian Neale went to work in Altrincham on MS for organic chemistry applications. A new MD was brought in, Alan Harrison, and a new Technical Director, Martin Elliot. Geoff Overend had arranged a trip to

South America and, as he was moving, asked me to step in. So at that point I felt secure in my position. I visited Caracas in Venezuela and Mexico City to visit geology departments and nuclear institutes. I had a weekend in Mexico City and visited Teotihuacán, a city built by a pre-Aztec civilisation and also the museum in the city dedicated to the countries pre-Hispanic past. The city did not seem intimidating or violent. I was out one morning walking through a park near the hotel. There was a shoe shine boy at a bench and I asked him how much. He got down to shining my shoes putting on a lot of polish. He then stood up and asked for twice the amount he had quoted. I protested but he shrugged and started to walk away. I had to pay him to avoid walking around with shoes well covered with polish.

The pricing issue was a general one for the group of companies because of fluctuating currency prices. I was told by Alan Harrison that there was to be a group meeting to discuss the issue. I did a quick report setting out what I believed was the best way forward – quoting in a number of currencies and different levels as discussed above. When people arrived for the meeting I started to go in and Craig said "I don't think we need you on this one, Bill". The meeting went ahead and then Harrison told me to his great amusement that he had put forward my proposal as his own and it had been accepted.

One night after just finishing a Chinese takeaway I had a phone call asking me to join Geoff Overend and Ian Neale for a meal and to meet the American agent, Gerry Kearns. I was a bit taken a back but went and had another meal with them. Kearns – like a lot of the VG management – had previously worked for AEI Scientific Instruments, in Trafford Park,

Manchester. When VG were getting going he had supported them by taking the agency for the USA. He said that he had to borrow money from his mother-in-law to set up in business and had an office in Stamford, Connecticut. He eventually did very well. I was a bit aggressive with him, suggesting new markets for the isotope instruments, but he took it very well and we became friends.

My new pricing policy really paid off – for example we got an order from Argentina for a stable isotope MS that would have been previously worth around £25,000, which came in for more than £40,000. Note that I had been aware that MAT also had a range of pricing based on where the customers were. The price did include an installation visit by and engineer and follow-up support. Sometimes the engineer spent several weeks getting the machine set up, especially if things got broken or failed after transit and parts had to be sent out from the UK.

I visited the US several times during this period, normally meeting Gerry Kearns and being accompanied by him to visit customers. The first trip actually started in Canada – Toronto, St Johns Newfoundland, Winnipeg, finally Victoria opposite Vancouver – with the Canadian agent. After that I transferred to Seattle to meet up with Gerry and Clive Haines for a Geochronology conference. One of the boffins, Tom Merren, also came. After they went back I travelled with Gerry to San Francisco for meetings. He looked after me well and we did some of the sights including having a drink at the "Top of the Mark" – the bar at the top of the Mark Hopkins hotel. We stayed at the Sir Francis Drake near to Union Square. We then moved to a motel in Palo Alto – the town where Varian and

Hewlett Packard were started, for meetings. It was also very close to Cupertino where Apple is based. At that time the term "Silicon Valley" had not come into use. Going back to the motel from San Francisco Gerry managed to run out of the petrol on the freeway. He free wheeled to an exit where we called for help.

We had a steady stream of business from agents but I dealt directly with East Bloc countries. I went to an exhibition in Moscow "Britnauchpribor" with Clive Haines. We had taken a thermal ionisation MS, but it turned out that the scientist who had secured the invitation wanted to buy a noble gas spectrometer. The confusion had arisen because another VG company had been to an exhibition there the year before and had spoken to the scientist but the message had got a bit garbled. At that time all trading with East Bloc countries was the monopoly of state companies who tended to be very bureaucratic. Geoff Overend had organised the trip prior to his move within VG – these things were always arranged years in advance.

Moscow was a bit miserable really and the horrible diesel they used for vehicles made you choke. The exhibition was in October. The customer had his funds for the instrument and I stayed on by myself for a further ten days. I would be called every few days for a meeting to discuss aspects of the deal. I ate in my hotel, the Ukraina, but found the hotel food pretty hopeless. They had a large menu but the only thing available on it was chicken Kiev. The waiter collected the money from you and then used it to pay for the food at the kitchen. Eventually I found by accident that there was a little snack bar hidden away on one of the upper floors and I would go there for ham and eggs.

There was a reception one night in a well-known restaurant called the Praga. When I came out there was a large queue for taxis and I decided to walk back to my hotel. It started to rain very hard and the temperature dropped. As I walked I realised I was lost and that there were a number of "Wedding Cake" type buildings like the Ukraina. I tried to ask people for directions but, as soon as I spoke, they realised I was a foreigner and took off. Eventually I came to the Moscow River and reasoned that if I turned right I would come to the Ukraina. I got back to the hotel very wet and cold. The next morning the whole city was covered in deep snow and I had a horrible sore throat (they called it Moscow throat). The change in climate was dramatic. From damp and cold as in England to very cold, overnight. The leaves on the trees had not had time to fall off and were frozen on. My throat eventually cleared up although I kept on coughing up green tubes! The contract was concluded and I returned to the UK.

Contracts like the Moscow one involved "letters of credit" in which the bank acted as an intermediary. You gave the bank the shipping documents once the instrument was packed and dispatched and they then sent the money. The engineer we sent to install the instrument had some problems. The hotel he stayed in caught fire and he lost all his belongings. Fortunately he had his passport; however when he came to return to the UK they detained him because he didn't match his passport photo. He had grown a beard in the meantime. The brief detention really shook the guy up.

M had been asked to make a sales visit to Japan. However, a few weeks before he was due to go he had a bad car accident. He drove into the back of a tanker. He was not wearing a seat belt and was thrown through the windscreen. Apparently, according to Alan Harrison, there was a large dent in the back of the tank where M had hit it with his head. It was decided that I should go instead to Japan. The agent set up the visits to prospects and generally looked after me – Bill san.

VG did have an entrepreneurial attitude to getting business and many of their products had started off as "specials" i.e. developed for a single specific customer. I adopted this with gusto. One of the areas I wanted to see developed was gas preparation systems. I thought the company would benefit from being able to offer labs a more complete package for isotope analysis. I had two main visits in Japan – to the Hot Springs Research Institute in the south of Hokaido and to a nuclear lab at Tskuba University. The former wanted to analyse hydrogen and oxygen isotope ratios on water samples and were interested in an automatic system including gas preparation equipment. The company was just starting to experiment with computers at this time. I took a chance really and quoted for the complete package and we got the contract. The Tsukuba order was for a thermal ionisation MS, also with computer data collection. MAT were the competitor and had just introduced a system that allowed multiple samples to be analysed without having to take the sample in and out of the vacuum chamber. It did this by rotation of the sample holder and could take 6 samples. I asked the engineer what was the maximum they thought we could offer and we came up with 13 and we again got the Japanese order.

I lost a lot of weight on that trip – the food was ok but in Japanese restaurants the food seemed to consist of something very tasty with soy sauce and pickles. Then a bowl of boiled rice, which I found it hard to eat by itself. However we had the occasional Chinese meal, which was more substantial. We had taken the bullet train to Osaka on our way to the institute and stayed the night in a Japanese Inn that had its own hot spring and bathing facilities. We were each given a small three-legged stool, a little wooden bucket, a small cloth and a bar of soap. You sat on the stool by the side of the pool, which was slightly raised and used your bucket to scoop out water to wash yourself with the soap. Once clean you entered the very hot pool. There were separate male and female pools.

I and the two Japanese men shared a room and we had tatami mats on the floor. One of the guys ground his teeth all night. The dining room had low tables and we sat on the floor. I quite liked the miso soup for breakfast. We travelled everywhere by train from Tokyo. My contact did have a car but it was only used to pick me up from the airport. Of course, everyone was very polite with lots of bowing. One a later trip we went by train to Akita in the north west of Hokkaido. It was an overnight sleeper train and they were too polite to alert me that the train was nearly there. I had no idea and couldn't read any of the signs. They had to wake me up and bundle me out onto the platform half-dressed and my suitcase in a bit of a mess.

I made quite a number of other trips abroad at this time including Czechoslovakia (big order for thermal ionisation MS) and Poland. A further trip took me Japan with visits to Taiwan and Philippines. I went to a Geochronology conference in

Snowmass, Colorado. I hired a car in Denver and drove there. Somehow on one of the winding roads through the Rockies I managed to cut out the engine – I think I was trying to force the automatic to a lower gear and put it into reverse. It was quite a big and heavy car and I lost power steering – quite a few heart-stopping moments followed as I went round the bends taking a lot of effort to turn the steering wheel. After the conference I was to fly to Australia for a conference in Brisbane. I flew Denver to Los Angeles and then caught the plane to Hawaii for an overnight stay. I remember enjoying a gin and tonic whilst looking down on the Grand Canyon with Gerry Rafferty's "Baker Street" playing on my headphones. I had a brief tour of Hawaii in a hire car but, when I got to the airport the following night, I found that I had got there a day late. I had misunderstood the timing of a flight to Sydney leaving just after midnight. I blamed it on the date line when I got to Brisbane a day late.

My last major overseas trip for VG was to Peking. The exhibition had been a year in the organising with pages of forms to fill in, visa applications etc. I was accompanied by M. We had a small stable isotope instrument with us. I had been producing newsletters for the company and in one issue I had floated the idea of us producing a commercial instrument for He^3/He^4 ratio analysis. Prior to that, scientists had produced their own in-house instruments. It became clear early on that they were not interested in the machine we had brought and they wanted to talk about the He^3/He^4 machine. A number of technical discussions took place and I dealt with queries by sending telexes back to Winsford. No doubt they read all the correspondence. Eventually I was called to a meeting and they said that they wanted to order a machine. Fortunately, I had already roughly priced up such an instrument, which we were the only ones offering, and factored in a "Chinese uplift". I had excluded Mike C. from the commercial negotiations for obvious reasons.

One evening we were invited to send a representative to a reception. I told M I was going and he kicked off saying he was the senior person. I stood my ground because I was well aware that the Chinese read a lot into how delegations were organised and I did not want my ability to negotiate undermined. I needed to maintain "face". He promised to "get me" when we got back to the UK.

I was asked to a further meeting and they said that they had good news! They wanted to order a further identical machine and required a "friendship discount". I gave them a further 5% off. The negotiator was a woman and at one of the meetings she managed to "accidently" let me see a copy of a quote I had done for a scientist at a university in Taiwan – obviously to try and show that they understood the pricing. The factory was now getting a bit excited as these were expensive instruments. I had a further final meeting where I was told that they had more good news for me! They wanted to order three instruments and wanted a further discount which I was able to give. I was required to stay in Peking for a further week after the exhibition closed so that contracts could be prepared and signed. It was a case of kicking my heels but I managed a sightseeing trip to the Great Wall, the Summer Palace and the Forbidden Palace. The exhibition was in October and it was extremely dry with dust storms from the Gobi Desert.

I had become interested in computing and asked the technical manager about the possibility of having some software written for my department. (I had an assistant by then). His response was to give me a book on the computer language BASIC and to get on with it!!! I wrote programs for producing pricing lists and then a mailing list editing and printing program. The latter was relatively complicated involving sorting of lists to put names and addresses into alphabetical order to make checking easier. At first, I used a DEC PDP8 then a HP desktop. I was taking the magazine *Scientific American* at the time and there was an issue concentrating on microcomputers.

My First Company 1979

Up until 1977, computers had specialist chip sets built by each manufacturer. However, a company called Intel had managed to get a full set of functions onto a single chip and put it on the market for applications such as controllers. When they launched their second-generation chip, 8080, it excited a lot of interest as the basis for complete computers. So-called microcomputers used these chips and added memory and interfaces. The initial micros were sold as kits for enthusiasts and had to be hand-programmed. Microsoft was formed to develop a BASIC interpreter for microcomputers. It allowed high level programming to take place. The Apple 2 was launched 16th April 1977.

I decided to start my own company. I had virtually no cash but contacted US producers including Apple to see if I could distribute their computers. I got a good response from a company called Ohio Scientific, which had introduced a range of cheap but advanced machines. I formed U-Microcomputers Ltd and bought one of Ohio Scientifics smallest computers as a demonstration model. I was working from home whilst still working for VG. I had a PO box number and got enquiries from PR to magazines and adverts. The pressure of working for VG and running another business was too much and I decided to leave VG. I had also closed some large orders (£8K +) for a couple of Ohio computers. I asked for 50% with order and 50% on delivery, so with these successfully installed I was in business.

Just before I left, I had another trip to Seattle and took the opportunity to visit a company called Seattle Computer

Products (SCP). They had produced a computer board with the first 16-bit microchip. I purchased one board as a demonstrator and took it home. It turned out that at that time IBM had decided to introduce its first microcomputer. It needed operating systems and they decided to offer users CP/M, p-system and one specifically for the IBM, PC-DOS. SCP had developed such a system for its hardware. Microsoft (by then in Seattle) had found out about this and bought the rights to the operating system, which they launched as MS-DOS. The deal with IBM was incredibly generous as it allowed Microsoft to sell other versions of PC-DOS to other hardware companies and the PC-compatible computer industry was launched. That was the nearest I ever came to meeting Bill Gates.

So I left VG and rented a small office in Weaverham near Northwich. VG had not wanted me to leave and I had several meetings with the directors. However, I really didn't want to work further with M. I think they may have wanted to offer me a more senior position but I must have seemed so adamant about doing my own thing that they never did. As you might expect M. made a number of difficulties when I left. I learned later that they had been unable to use the mailing list program although I had left it in a good state. I had offered to do some consultancy for them to generate a bit of cash, but they refused. It was their loss really.

The summer before I left, I did my first long-distance walk. I had been going to start a model railway but sold the track I had bought and went to do the first half of the Offa's Dyke long-distance path. Anne took me down to Monmouth where I stayed in a B&B and then set off the next morning. I had little idea of what it involved. I had walked locally but only a couple of miles and thought I was generally fit. I took books to read and used an old ex-army rucksack I had bought and used as a student in London. It had been to Germany with me when we went up the Zugspitze. I quickly found that it was much too heavy and, the next day, packed up a load of stuff and posted it home! The rucksack had a metal frame and that rubbed into me. I had a plan but found I had made the stages too long. I phoned each day to arrange my accommodation.

The first stage was relatively flat, so the first real climb was when I arrived at the Black Mountains for the walk to Hay on Wye. As the day wore on I decided that was too far and came down into Llanthony to stay the night. I got to Hay the next night and, as I was walking, I met up with another walker who was camping. He had previously walked the Ridgeway in the south of England and we met up a few times. Kington and Knighton followed. I had a real struggle with the hill out of Knighton and felt that I had really run out of energy. I was aiming for Montgomery but decided that was too far and came off the path to stay the night in Bishops Castle. I enjoyed a nice steak in a pub there. I then travelled back home by bus and train to Northwich.

The following year I was determined to complete the path armed with a better knowledge of myself and my equipment. I started in Montgomery and finished in Prestatyn from where I caught the train home. There was a long break then before I did serious walking again.

U-Microcomputers Ltd. 1979–1989

So, I went into business on my own and formed U-Microcomputers Ltd in June 1979. Anne and I had had our first daughter, Elizabeth, in October 1977 and we were due another child in September 1979. So, there was a lot to cope with all at once for both of us. I was delivering a computer to the Isle of Man when Anne went into labour at Leighton Hospital near Crewe and we had a daughter we named Joanna.

Ohio Scientific had announced a new product called "Superboard 2" that looked extremely attractive. It was an integrated board with keyboard and I had some plans to box the board up for sale with power supply etc. However the launch date kept on being put back. I never found out the reason but I suspect that they were already overwhelmed with orders for more expensive products. In the end a small company in London copied the board (and got a software licence for Microsoft BASIC) and for a short while swept the market.

Ohio appointed a company called American Data to handle their sales to Europe. The prices went up a bit and the opportunity to be the importer and to appoint sub-distributors was lost. Pricing consisted of doubling the US price and calling it pounds so, for a short while, margins were high. This later encouraged discounting as others tried to jump on the bandwagon. I had major problems with reliability on the Ohio products and employed a couple of engineers on a freelance basis. On one occasion, I had a new computer in for a client and was checking it out, including making back-up floppy discs. As I tested the new disks I found that although the copying had seemed to go OK, the new disks would not boot up. I had one good master disc left when I called a halt and asked the engineer to come by. He looked at the disc controller board and thought that a few of the soldered connections look bad, so he re-soldered them all. The machine then worked. Otherwise, I would have had to get a new computer from the USA along with new discs. Nightmare.

Apple

I decided to take on another product to make the business more robust. Apple had just appointed a UK distributer based in Hemel Hempstead and launched an updated version of the Apple 2. You had to buy two computers with disk drives to join their program. My father said he wanted to help and agreed to buy one of the Apples for his own use. Apple then became the main focus. There was UK support and the quality of the product was much higher. One of the early big orders was from a firm of surveyors in Knutsford. It included a daisywheel printer, which actually cost more than the Apple. I ordered in all the items and then phoned the customer to arrange to deliver and set up. I had a few things on that week and I put off the delivery till the following week. I phoned to confirm the delivery and they told me that they had ordered an ITT2020 from a competing dealer. So I was stuck with the specialist printer (and the Apple computer). The lesson was clear – get the stuff out the door ASAP. The 2020 was a version of the Apple 2 made by ITT under licence and was a problem for a short while. It wasn't developed further and didn't benefit from the various things that Apple introduced in the way of accessories and software, so it fell by the wayside.

I employed a secretary to answer the phone and manage the office better. She must have mentioned this to her husband. He was a manager at Ince B power station down on the Wirral. I had a few chats with him about him getting involved in the business. Coincidently, I had a guy drop in called Tony Smith who lived in Cuddington and he asked about the Apple. He came back a week later and said that he might be interested in investing in the business as an active partner. He had sold a business a couple of years ago in the waste management field. In the end I felt that this was the best way forward as it is difficult running a business without any assistance. He introduced me to his former finance director and made me an offer – 51% of the business for the net asset value of the business. The cash was for new shares and a loan and hence invested in the business. I had kept rudimentary books and from this the finance guy came up with £9000. This was less than my back-of-an-envelope calculation of profit made on each sale less expenses. I had not taken any salary for the first couple of months and run up my credit card to live on. In the early days, my main calculation had been how long I could go for without running out of cash if no more orders came in. So the net asset value represented entirely retained profit, which was pretty good for a one-man band in roughly 6 months.

However, this raises the issue of how do you value a business? Once established it is more usual to value it on a multiple of annual profits (and even a multiple of turnover in some high growth business). My understanding of accounts and issues such as valuation was poor at the time, but I realised that I had to get to grips with accounts. Anyway, I accepted Tony's offer and we were also able to move into some office units in Long Lane, Warrington, which was part of an industrial estate Tony owned. I would have been afraid to make such a move by myself because of the greater overheads. We installed a telephone answering machine and also got a new part-time secretary of Tony's previous acquaintance.

We dropped Ohio altogether to concentrate on Apple. I was doing all the demos and Tony was helping and doing admin. He of course wanted to expand the business and we employed a new salesman called Roy Stringer. He had worked for one of the very first computer shops in Liverpool and knew the Apple well. He was an excellent salesman and sales increased.

During 1980, we decided to move to Warrington for me to be nearer to work and we bought a four-bedroom, modern house in Cinnamon Brow. Nicky had just started at junior school in Hartford, so it was a good time to move. The children all went to the same primary/junior school in Cinnamon Brow.

We started to be held back by Apple appointing all and sundry as dealers and there was no exclusivity of sales area. We sold across the north west down to Wolverhampton and across north Wales to Bangor where the university was a good customer. I came to the conclusion that our potential was being severely limited. I tried a few things, including writing a stock control program for the Apple and sold a few copies. I must have noticed in the computer mags that people were starting to import memory boards for the Apple from the US. A new opportunity! I contacted an engineer from VG that I had been friends with – he had been quite supportive when I left – and asked him to do a printed circuit board (PCB) layout. There was no software involved in the PCB so no real copyright issues. I then contacted local companies making PCBs and had a small batch made. The prototype worked well, so with Tony's agreement I went ahead and ordered 100 PCBs. I also asked a contact in the VG buying dept. where they sourced their electronic components from and arranged with that company for them to supply complete kits of parts, as I did not want a complicated stock control problem.

Apple published a list of their dealers, so I put that into a mailing list and offered the new 16K memory board – "U-RAM 16". They sold out almost immediately and so we were in business. I used outworkers to assemble the boards and employed an engineer to test them. I designed the packing and did a little user manual to complete the package. In the end we sold over 10,000 U-RAM 16.

Wozniak had designed the Apple to be uniquely expandable with 6 slots at the back to take expansion boards. This was, I believe, at the heart of its success as it allowed the product to advance with Apple not having to redesign the computer frequently. Of course Steve Jobs hated Apple not having complete control of the package being sold and he made machines like the Macintosh basically unexpandable. Many more boards were added to our catalogue and the company grew rapidly. We continued to be an Apple dealer but made much higher margins by putting our own cards into the machines we sold.

We expanded our premises to include a lot more space, including areas that had not been let in the past, for offices and ground floor space for manufacturing. We continued to subcontract the assembly of the boards and eventually started to get more professional with a cleaning plant to remove flux from the assembled boards. Our test procedure was pretty basic – plug it into an Apple and see if it worked. As the pile of non-working boards grew we had to employ engineers to repair the boards so that they could be sold.

One of the early Apple customers had been designers of power controls for electric motors based in Northwich. They moved to Skelmersdale and got a large contract from a major company making copper wire. The factory melted copper and squirted it through a die and, as the jet cooled, it formed copper wire. There were large electric motors that drove and controlled the process. Our customer had got into difficulties and the MD, David Brash, asked us if we would help them out. We knew nothing about the business but, on the face of it, it seemed to be a business with big potential.

The company went into liquidation and we did a deal with the liquidator to take it over and formed U-Power Systems. After many more months of effort and the system not working we had to pull the plug and let Dave Brash go. When he started with us he asked if a former employee of his could join the company and, as it happened, we were recruiting a production manager. This guy turned out to be a bit of a disaster. We had a visit from a company that was a scientific journal publisher that wanted to get into the microcomputer business. He wanted a batch of boards to send to his German office to replicate the distribution model we were using in the UK – i.e. sell to Apple dealers. He gave us an order for £10,000 worth of boards. I was reluctant to accept the order because he wanted immediate delivery. The production manager said that we could do it and we dispatched the order. Almost immediately boards were returned. They decided to test the whole batch themselves and most of them came back. We never had another order from Germany and, shortly afterwards, I sacked the production manager. He had just packed up boards without testing and sent them out.

When I started U-Micro I saw it as one of a group of businesses using small computer technologies. U-Power Systems was not of course directly related. One other business I started was U-Sci Limited with a brief to develop software for data collection from scientific instruments. I poached a guy from VG's software dept. and we specified software for data collection from gas chromatographs with Apple computers. An interface boards was developed for us – U-A/D – an analogue to digital converter board. It turned out to be a long-term seller in its own right.

I got the first order from Lancaster University. We even employed a second software guy from VG to develop the infrared spectrometer software. U-Sci then got a development contract to do a version of the software for the Apricot computer – this was a briefly successful MS-DOS computer that was not IBM-compatible. Included was the development of a processing board based on the Apple design but with two microprocessors. Although the development was eventually completed, it took a lot of resource away from the other U-Sci products and the business did not really thrive. The market was there however and a Swiss company that had been founded by the Varian European Sales Manager, of my acquaintance, based in Zug was very successful. It was eventually purchased by Perkin Elmer, a leading US instrument company.

At this time we also opened an office in Stamford, Connecticut run by Gerry Kearns' son, Jack. It had limited success because the Taiwanese got into the market for Apple add-ons and made us uncompetitive in the USA. Looking back on that period, I spread my effort much too widely, too many products, not enough in-house expertise etc. We also launched a range of IBM pc memory cards but bigger companies were rapidly into that market and we only did moderately well. The Apple add-ons market had kind of happened spontaneously and we were the first to get off the ground in the UK. Other well-funded start-up UK competitors entered the market but they struggled to compete. We even ended up buying up the stock of a company that was based in north Wales after they failed. They produced real-time clock and voice boards that we sold off but never manufactured ourselves.

Our sales peaked at around £800,000 pa and we embarked on even more ambitious product developments. The Sinclair Spectrum had come out and we thought that, like the Apple, it would create a market for add-ons. The customer we had at Bangor University suggested the products and we produced quite a nice range of interface add-ons. Sinclair however made some serious product mistakes. He promised a tape-based storage device as a low-cost alternative to floppy discs. This product never really materialised. They also miscalculated the market at Christmas for the Spectrum and got into financial difficulty, so the company failed. The computer was only on the market for a relatively short time.

Development and Manufacture of Computers

We developed an "Apple Compatible" board that initially I saw selling to people incorporating the Apple into equipment (which included scientific instruments). We asked the guys at Bangor to develop the ROM (read only memory) – which contained the only software on the board and hence copyright. The prototypes worked well and sales started to look promising. However, we had major reliability problems as the design turned out to be very sensitive to which memory chips were included. The in-house expertise was poor at the time and it took probably a year to get the problems worked out. We lost a large contract from a company called Country Computers who wanted to box up the board to compete directly with Apple. Needless to say, Apple were not very happy with us but did not terminate our dealership arrangement. By this time Apple had bought out the UK distributor. They did poach our prize salesman Roy Stringer.

We also embarked on the development of a computer using the Motorola 68000 chip – a promising 16-bit chip that we hoped would allow us to move forward as the Apple 2 declined. We got a government grant for this but subcontracted the development to an engineer who had worked on the BBC micro with Acorn Computers. He wanted to build a computer like the BBC micro but with almost every function built in. We asked him to include an Apple-compatible slot system to allow for expansion. The development took way longer than expected, but we eventually went into production. It turned out to be an expensive machine and we opted to sell models with hard discs included, with floppy just for back up. In the end, we rejigged the design of the computer to give us a single computer board and a separate interfaces board. We had some good orders for it. But our U-MICRO Series1000 computer had missed its moment and the IBM PC and compatibles were dominating the market. The market for more powerful workstations went to Sun and Silicon Graphics with UNIX machines.

The Apple add-on cards business started to decline. Very cheap boards started to come in from Taiwan. The complete board sold for less than we could buy the components. The Apple 2 lasted longer than anyone expected. Apple introduced the Apple 3, which had built-in hard disc and more memory. Then came the Apple Lisa which caused quite a stir, but it was an overblown product – their first with a mouse (and used the 68000 processor). The Mackintosh arrived but the first models were very limited with floppy only and it only gradually made headway.

We had a networking product for the Apple 2 called U-NET, which allowed sharing of printers and storage. A guy from Lancaster University had designed it. We sold about 50 sets to schools.

As mentioned, we had by now a good development team but our products had come to market a bit late. The future was not all that clear and, in the end, Tony Smith and I parted company. I had kept in touch with Robert Craig at VG and he suggested to colleagues that maybe they should invest in a computer company. This was not as odd as it sounds because Varian had bought a small computer start-up many years before and of course Hewlett-Packard had branched out from instruments into computers. The deal with VG gave me extra capital and they asked us to develop an interface board for a range of instrumentation for gas analysis. Funnily enough, they were already a customer for our Apple-compatible product.

We had joined a trade association – British Microcomputer Manufacturers Group – which had been formed to promote the industry. The ludicrous situation had arisen where government procurement rules meant that government departments could not buy from British manufacturers. I was on the committee and we had a meeting with Kenneth Baker, one of Mrs Thatcher's favourites. We were discussing the time it took to get decisions on government grants, with one of our members complaining. I was nodding at this and Baker said "What are you nodding your head for" in an aggressive way. I said that we also had to wait many months and he said to his minder "Look into this for me". Of course, I never heard anymore. I became chairman for a while and, as a result, was invited to a garden party at Buckingham Palace. It was an odd kind of event, with most of us milling around (nice sandwiches) with a select group meeting the Queen and royal family in a cordoned-off enclosure. Notables on our side were Jeremy Thorpe, notorious when leader of the Liberal party for trying to have his gay ex-lover killed, and Dennis Healey former Labour Chancellor of the Exchequer.

I felt that things were maybe not going to go well when, at the first meeting with Jim Ramage from VG, whose remit we fell under, I was asked "Your new computer is IBM-compatible isn't it?" Of course it was not! The U-Sci business was also struggling and I decided to do a deal with the developer for him to buy that business off us.

We took on the sale of some chemical modelling software developed by a couple of guys at Glasgow University to help sell our 6800 based computer. We turned it into a dedicated modelling workstation with our own hardware and, at £15000 a time with good margins, it started to do quite well.

After about six months it was apparent that we were not going to grow as fast as hoped and VG decided to pull the plug – they didn't want liquidation and they asked me how much I would pay them for their shares. The negotiations were over the phone with the company secretary. I told them that I could find £4000 and that was it and would need the several hundreds of thousands of pounds they had loaned the business to be turned into a long-term loan. They hummed and hawed and, in the end, I said that I had had enough – I wanted to take a few weeks holiday and then I would return and help them liquidate the business. They backed down and a deal was done, including sales of our Apple-compatible mother board and orders for the interface board we had developed for them. The interface board development had been a major effort; it did not result in further sales, and delayed further development of our own computer.

The year after VG pulled out actually turned out to be excellent for sales and, at one point, we had £100,000 in the bank. Of course the bank then tried to get me to increase my personal overdraft, which fortunately I didn't do. We moved to modern premises on Winwick Quay, quite close to our previous premises in Long Lane.

The following year, 1989, saw the end of U-Micro. A few things contributed. We were an IBM PC dealer and that was also plagued by discounting. You would do the work for the sale and then be undercut – and then the customer would be back onto you for technical support.

We had one disastrous larger sale with multiple PCs. It took up a lot of time after the sale and, unfortunately, the sales person had promised things which we could not deliver, so that came back. We had done a development for a small firm in Oxford that had a contract with British American Tobacco. It involved a system to collect results from customer panels being quizzed on cigarettes for their marketing department. The development had been completed and a large order had been placed with us and delivered to them. BAT rejected the project and our customer went into liquidation, leaving us with large unpaid invoices. The cards business was still OK. Repaying the loans to VG was another major burden.

We had completed by that summer another version of our computer, this time with the more powerful 68020 chip. I had also got us on the Transputer bandwagon. This was a British designed chip that aimed to drastically speed up computing power by allowing processors to operate in parallel. We built a new graphics board around it to go with our computer and make a very powerful chemical modelling workstation. We also produced a 16 Transputer board for the most intensive modelling computations.

We were never able to benefit from these products. Overheads had been cut back but we were overstretched financially. The bank was requiring monthly accounts. We had a £20,000 overdraft with the bank that we were fully utilising and, out of the blue, they called me in and demanded that I guarantee the overdraft with a charge over our house. A large cheque had just come in reducing the overdraft to zero but giving us no cash for wages or suppliers. I refused and they told me to call in a liquidator. So that was that. I had lost confidence in the bank and was afraid that they could not be trusted to support the business. We were not alone in being in that situation at the time and there was a bit of a depression that lasted until 1994/95. One of the contacts I had, in a similar business, told me that when they had had a rough patch they omitted to give the bank the full picture and gradually turned the business round. So my lesson there was never to trust the banks. We had a disgraceful similar thing happen much later in 2006.

I am ashamed and still very angry with something else that happened at that time and definitely contributed to demise of the business. From about the second year of U-Micro we had employed a full-time accountant who had previously worked for Tony Smith. Without me really noticing, he had gradually built up a team of young girls to do the paperwork. When Craig had looked at the business prior to the VG takeover he had remarked that there seemed to be a lot of young girls running around the place. Looking back, I don't think that there was anything inappropriate going on and there were no complaints. The accountant left after the VG takeover and the accounting function moved to one of the VG subsidiaries.

When I got control back I didn't really change the policy. One day, about 4 months before the business failed, I got a phone call from a researcher at a college in Oxford complaining that she had asked for leaflets and price list on our A/D interface system for the IBM PC and she had not received them. I made a note and passed it down to the female receptionist. She was only sixteen or seventeen and I must have recruited her or maybe someone else did. She seemed to be coping with the job but had just become pregnant. A few weeks later I got another phone call from the same person, this time very irate saying she still had not received the leaflets. I apologised, made another note of her details and went downstairs to check.

I asked to see the outstanding enquires. She opened the bottom drawer of her desk and it was full of paper. Handwritten telephone requests for leaflets plus pages of leads from advertising and PR in magazines. I was totally appalled as we had put a lot of effort and money into advertising new products and sending out press releases. We had spent thousands on high quality colour leaflets. The leads went back three months or so. There was no point in berating the girl. I immediately told most of the office and sales staff to drop what they were doing and got them typing up address labels and stuffing envelopes with the appropriate leaflets. A day's work by three or four of us (including me) cleared the backlog. However I am sure that it caused the loss of a lot of business. After that I didn't employ youngsters, which was a pity in some ways.

I went to see the company accountant, Peter Jeffries, and he suggested we ask a firm in Manchester called Poppleton and Appleby to be liquidators. He advised me not do anything that I might regret later. There was a brief pause when the bank had second thoughts and asked a firm of accountants from Liverpool to have a look at whether the business could be saved. They came for a day and were getting organised when there was a call that the bank had changed its mind and they pulled out. The liquidators took charge and told me they would pay me cash to work for them for a month to help with the liquidation. The staff were dismissed but got statutory redundancy payments from the state fund. This actually included me and, being the longest serving employee, I got the most. My wife Anne, who had been an employee, also got a sum of money. Both the family cars were leased and they were repossessed by the finance company so I had to get my bike out.

I had not made much money out of the business except for a reasonable salary since about the second year. Starting the company had not really been about money. In the two years that I had got back control of the company from VG I had started a directors' pension scheme and invested £10,000 each year. I had put £4000 back into the company as share capital when taking back control. I think that after ten years I was tired of running the business. Some key people left in the final period when the situation became strained. I, of course, could not. Owning a small business can be a bit of a trap.

In the month of winding up we had calls from customers to place orders including a pretty substantial one from Ferranti (Defence contractors) and from the Ferring Research Institute near Portsmouth. We had an order from Czechoslovakia for a chemical modelling system for the PC – not involving our own hardware and I briefly considered diverting it to dormant U-Sci Limited and fulfilling the order to make about £3000, but I followed Peter Jeffries' advice. The development engineers were very upset when the technical drawings, circuit diagrams and PCB layouts all went into the skip – they represented many man years of work.

Sailing

Here is another digression! During the 80s I had taken up sailing as a hobby. I had been interested for quite a while and even Jenny and I had had a go during the 60s. A previous boyfriend of hers, Brendan, had been a keen sailor. My father had taken up dingy sailing after her death. I went out with him a few times on a dinghy he had bought and took to Grafham Water near Bedford.

My first experience was on a course at the National Sailing centre at Cowes on the Isle of Wight in 1984. It was a six-day course, first near the Isle of Wight and then a cross-channel sail to Alderney and Cherbourg. We did a night crossing of the channel on our return. It was a life-enhancing experience. I decided not to buy a boat as I knew I could only give it a week or two each year. In 1985 I sailed with the Ocean Youth Club as trainee mate on the Sir Francis Drake – Peel, Portpatrick, Portrush, Bangor, Ardglesh, Douglas, and Holyhead. We had a group of young people from London as the crew. 1986 saw me doing my day skipper course from Plas Menai in Wales – Port Dinorwic, Conway, Moelfre, Cemaes Bay, Holyhead, Menai Bridge and back to Port Dinorwic. The emphasis was on coming into harbour in different circumstances under sail, under power, different wind and tide situations.

I did my coastal skipper course in 1987, again starting from Port Dinorwic – Holyhead, Port St Mary, Douglas, Cemaes Bay, Beaumaris. This required passage planning and acting as captain for a day. For two years I also attended the theory courses at Riverside College in Liverpool. The RYA/DTI certificates required passes in both the practical and theory courses and required a cumulative number of nights on boat, distance sailed and night sailing hours. To obtain the yacht master qualification would have meant spending much more time at sea – time that I didn't have. I had however logged over a 1000 miles at sea. I did a bit more sailing in north Wales and in Scotland in 1988 and 1989 but then didn't do any more until 1999 after I sold my business.

After U-Micro 1989

So, after a brief break helping the liquidators, I had to move
on. I went to see the building society to discuss my mortgage
and they turned it into interest only. I decided to try and avoid
buying a car and to stop all unnecessary expenditure.

It seemed to me that the best way to proceed would be to try
and get a job in sales and marketing. I didn't have the money
or the will to start in business again and maybe a corporate life
would suit me. I went to agencies and, at one, I got some tough
but necessary advice – not to "wear my heart on my sleeve"
i.e. potential new employers would not want to hear all about
my trials and tribulations at U-Micro. I had interviews with
people like Sun Microsystems and things were moving along.

I was offered an interview in London with a firm called DBMS,
which did software for large businesses running big software
systems on IBM mainframe computers. The guy I met was their
European manager and he was German. I started the interview
by saying "Wie gehts?" which threw him straight away as he
did not expect to meet someone who spoke a bit of German.
The rest of the interview was in English but the impression was
made. Although the company was located in London they were
just about to move to new offices in Reading. The salary and
sales commission package looked good and there was a nice
company car, so I took the offer. I had signed on for
unemployment benefit and ended up claiming for only one
month. At the benefit sign-on the interviewer had said – "I
don't think we will see you around for long", which was
another boost to my confidence.

I decided to stay with my mother and father in Bedford and commute to Reading. I also expected to be out in the field visiting customers. It turned out that DBMS would have paid my expenses to stay in a hotel as with some of the other employees who needed to move house following the move from central London.

My father had stayed for many years with GF and he had been passed over for promotion after the Swiss senior management he had got on with retired. He got a management job with a metal castings company in Keighley around the time I started U-Micro. We visited him at a little flat there once. He then moved on to work for a company called Micro Metal Smiths based in Kirkby Moorside on the edge of the York moors. He seemed to settle in there and they bought a new house on the edge of the town. We went there quite a few times and stayed. Andrew had moved with them and he had gone to college not that far away in Middlesbrough. Martin had moved in with his girlfriend Nicola in Bedford and later they were married.

My mum and dad were quite full of Christopher Shaw, the owner, who had a big house on the edge of the moors. My father had an Audi Quattro as a company car. I don't know why things turned sour, but he lost the job there and they decided to move back to Bedford. House prices had turned against them with big increases in the south east but not in Yorkshire. They ended up getting a much smaller house than before, in Putnoe, just round the corner from Greenacres. My mother went into a real depression and we were very worried about her. I don't know what went on between the three of them (i.e. including Andrew) and I was even asked to employ Andrew at U-Micros for a while to get him away from my father. In the end they moved again, out of Bedford to a village called Bromham and that is where they were when I stayed with them.

My sister also eventually settled in Bromham. She was a teacher and had worked in London and then as a headteacher in Bedfordshire.

I travelled back and forth to Warrington at weekends and commuted daily to Reading when I needed to be in the office. Most of the money that DBMS made came from maintenance contracts on the software and it was a struggle to get any new business. I visited existing customers and tried to get new business from other users of IBM systems. IBM had introduced their own database system called DB2 and DBMS had launched their own add-on products. I only got one order in the months I worked there – for a British Telecomms associated company in Singapore. I got the order just before I left and they honoured their commission agreement.

So I realised it was a bit of a dead end, but didn't actually start looking for another job. However, I had had an interview at Morgan Crucible Plc at their head office in Windsor before accepting the DBMS job. They had funded a start-up based in Swansea at their manufacturing plant. Things had gone quiet but, after I started at DBMS, they got in touch again and I had a further interview in Swansea with a guy called Mike Rosser. He had run Corgi Toys before it had been sold to Mattel and was now owner of and running a plastics moulding company in Swansea. He was an experienced businessman.

A heart surgeon, working in Cardiff, had designed a new mechanical heart valve. They had needed a new technology to manufacture it and, by coincidence, were put in touch with a professor at Swansea who had been working with a material called glassy carbon. It was made by heating up a mouldable resin to high temperature in the absence of oxygen. It had been decided to use this technology to fabricate the surgeon's valve. They wanted an MD for the company and I seemed to fit the bill. Because they took so long to make their mind up, I suspect in retrospect that they had found it difficult to recruit someone who was already experienced in the medical implants field. However I took it that Morgan Crucible had done their due diligence on the company and were attracted to it because carbon products such as carbon crucibles for metal smelting and pantographs for railways were their main business. I had run a small business and maybe I could become a small cog in a much bigger one. So I resigned from DBMS, who were not too pleased I was leaving after such a short time.

Swansea – Cardio Carbon Company Limited (CCCL) 1990–1994

So I headed for Swansea. I stayed in a Holiday Inn hotel for a while. Cardio Carbon had been allocated offices in a small block at the Morriston factory of Morganite. We had a couple of rooms upstairs and quite a large laboratory downstairs. The other employee was a Ph.D. from Swansea who had done the research on glassy carbon. He had ordered equipment before I arrived and initially it was a question of setting up the lab and offices. There was a high temperature furnace, moulding machine and other laboratory equipment. We both had Dell computers upstairs. The other occupant of the offices was a company developing electronic sensors for portable instruments such as carbon monoxide monitors. I was to report to a John Seymour who had interviewed me in Windsor at their head office where he was based. At the time of the interview, I was also seen by another main board director and I asked him what he actually did! He was surprised by the question and was not really able to answer!

Seymour had previously been the MD of the Morganite plant in Swansea and one of the things he said was to see his ex-secretary if I needed any typing doing. She did one letter for me, but made it pretty clear working for me was beneath her. So it was then that I learnt to type using a PC program I bought.

I was encouraged to find that the company already had a trial order from a company called Medtronic Inc. from Minneapolis for a carbon component for their mechanical heart valve. The valve consisted of a carbon disc in a metal cage and it had been on the market for a while using another form of carbon called pyrolytic carbon.

This was produced by depositing carbon vapour on graphite former. It was an expensive method because the disk had to be machined and polished after the deposition process. We aimed to mould a resin and carbonise it so that it needed no further processing, hence reducing cost. The moulding machine arrived with the mould for the Medtronic disc and we went into production and sent a small batch to them. We were invited over to discuss the results with them. This was in February 1990 – and Minneapolis was the coldest place I have ever been to! The test results were not good – the discs had all shattered in the test rig. Glassy carbon was known to be brittle, but this was a major setback. Contractions of the heart open and close the valves and when the flow reverses the valve closes rapidly. People with heart valves can hear a distinct "click" so the force is considerable.

We produced another batch of samples but with the same result, so it wasn't a particular batch problem but a design issue. The design of the valve had been finalised and we had a mould produced for that. It worked quite differently from other valves. It had two leaves, each leaf having two hinges in a carbon housing. So there were a number of components to be produced and it took quite a while to get it all together. At the same time I initiated contacts with various overseas and UK distributors and went on a number of overseas visits with the surgeon. Because we knew that the approvals process for the valve would take a long time, we developed a much simpler product called a valvuloplasty ring, which was used for valve repair rather than replacement. The market was limited and we would compete with titanium implants that were covered in cloth. Our ring was glassy carbon with holes for sutures and we considered it would have higher biocompatibility than competitor products. I also applied for innovation grants to help us develop other implants made from glassy carbon.

Initially I got a small flat in the centre of Swansea. It was in Paxton Court and was a new purpose-built set of flats facing onto Oystermouth Road. It was near by the marina. It was a bit noisy during the rush hour but, of course, I was normally not there then. I drove home to Warrington every weekend. On Friday night I went cross-country via Newtown but on a Sunday evening I used the M5/M50.

We had already put the house in Warrington on the market and signed up for a new house just outside Swansea in Penclawdd. The sale in Warrington was very protracted and the buyer kept stringing things along and asking for discounts. The effect of this on the family was not great and, in the end, we completed the sale just the week of the start of the autumn school term. So there was no chance for the children to get used to where they were going. Elizabeth started senior school and went to Gowerton School on the edge of Swansea. It had a reputation as a good school. Joanna went to the local junior school in Penclawdd. Both had to learn Welsh as a second language. It turned out that Jo was quite behind the standard there and had a lot of catching up to do. The estate of new houses, Waun-y-Felin, was on the way to Swansea and on the north Gower overlooking the Loughor estuary. There was a wide expanse of water across to the Llanelli side. Directly in front of us was a large marshland area that just looked like an expanse of meadow. Locally owned horses ran free. However, when you went down onto the marsh it was criss-crossed by deep channels. The tide filled these each day and, on a spring tide, the grass completely disappeared leaving the horses stranded with their legs in the water. They had to keep still then because of the channels. Further down the estuary to the west the marshland was replaced by large areas of sand and mud. The estuary was harvested for cockles, a local delicacy.

I think that Anne and I would have been able to settle there, but Liz fell out with the school and we had all sorts of problems. Jo made friends with local children. I went with her one bonfire evening to a friend's house just along towards Penclawdd. There was a wrecked boat on the marsh that belonged to the father. He said it had beached on a spring tide and had then been vandalised. They had a barbecue and were cooking sardines as the fireworks went off. Anne joined the local choir and fitted in. The local neighbours were a mixture of English incomers like us and local Welsh people. One was a bank manager. Another was a nurse who had been working in the Gulf for the local military and had left the area without authorisation during the First Gulf War. She was afraid of being arrested if she went back. She claimed that she had had a boyfriend who worked for the SAS who had been killed on a mission.

My favourite walk was from Llangennith to Rhossili along the downs and back along the beach. The rest of the family showed no interest in walking unfortunately. In the summer we enjoyed the beaches. The first Christmas most of the rest of the family turned up – my mother and father, sister Margaret and husband and brother Andrew. Somehow, they were all fitted into the four-bedroom house. I had a short commute to

Morriston, either through an older part of Swansea or via the M4.

The prototype valves were sent to a valve-testing laboratory in Sheffield run by one of the UK experts in the field. The test rigs pumped water back and forth, opening and closing the valve at an accelerated rate. They tested over months the wear experienced over years. If a valve failed, nothing could be done and the recipient died almost immediately – hence the emphasis on simulated long-term trials. These trials seemed to go ok. The next step was to prepare for animal trials. The surgeon used his contacts to arrange for implantation in pigs in the Netherlands. Unfortunately, the valves shattered and the trial was a failure. It was decided to revise the design and strengthen the hinges. They were a potential problem because any part of the valve that wasn't flushed during each cycle could potentially cause blood clots. For the next series of trials the surgeon implanted them into a sheep – he did the operation himself. Unfortunately, the new valves also shattered, putting the whole project in doubt. The valvuloplasty rings had completed development and, on his own responsibility, the surgeon had used them on patients with good results. (It was perfectly legal for a surgeon to do this on a limited scale.) The surgeon had in the meantime moved from Cardiff to Bristol and joined the heart team there. This is where the Bristol heart surgery scandal had arisen with the paediatric team showing very poor outcomes and sacking the whistle-blower. He had been blackballed in the UK and had to go to Australia to find a job. They got their comeuppance as the scandal unfolded and an enquiry was launched.

Without the heart valve there was no viable business. I started looking for jobs again and decided, if possible, to get one in the north west and move back to Warrington. I had several interviews at this time.

I started to think of alternative business ventures in Swansea. I rejected a potato delivery round I saw in the paper as lacking in potential! The Welsh Development Agency and Swansea had set up trade links with the south west of France and I looked into starting a food and wine importing business. We had a holiday booked to the Loire area and whilst there I took the opportunity of driving to Pau in France to see some potential suppliers. I came back with wine, pate, jams, honey and whole foie gras. We had the neighbours around when we got back for a tasting session. I didn't take this idea forward.

On my own initiative, I started to see if there as an alternative way of making the valve. Pyrolytic carbon was not an option because of the complexity of the design. In the end I settled on looking into a device made of titanium for strength but coated with a new form of carbon – diamond like carbon - for enhanced biocompatibility and resistance to wear. A titanium-only implant would have worn at the hinges and failed. This was a very drastic change of direction.

The business plan supported by Morgan Crucible was already way out of date. We had had to ask for more money a couple of times and I had sold in advance the distribution rights to several overseas distributors to raise cash. I had contacted my old flat mate, Nigel Weselby, who was working for a medical company in Brighton as their Middle East export manager. We had tendered for a few orders for valvuloplasty rings without success. We had attempted to develop other carbon implants using our development grants. We had even employed a young researcher and a lab technician but these developments had not been successful. During this time I had become a small shareholder in the business.

When Morgan Crucible was presented with a new business plan they rejected it immediately. However, they did not want the bad publicity of closing the firm down and, in the end, a deal was reached that I, the surgeon and our medical marketing expert should take over the business with an injection of cash from Morgan Crucible. I was given a lump sum on leaving, provided I invested it in the business, which I did. There was no particular point in staying in Swansea, so the staff were all made redundant and I relocated to Warrington. The surgeon was in Bristol, the marketing guy on the south coast, the titanium fabrication company was in Luton and the carbon coating was to be done by a group at Nottingham University.

Back To Warrington 1994

So I escaped from Swansea and, although a beautiful place, it would have been (like Margate) a career dead end. The move went smoothly and I had agreed to take a small salary to look after Cardio Carbon's project. This meant that I was able to do other things and I got a number of marketing contracts with instrument related companies in the north west. When I moved I went in to see the personnel manager at Morganite and explained the situation and asked if I could list Morganite as my employer in applying for a mortgage and he agreed. We were able to move to a similar house rather than a drastic downsize and I converted the garage into an office, installing phone, computer and fax and putting up plastic sheeting to be able to keep a small part of the garage warm.

I went for interviews but I started to doubt the wisdom of working for someone else again and started putting out feelers to start another business. I spoke to the man who had been the senior engineer at U-Micro about starting a new business manufacturing cards and add-ons for portable PCs, which were just hitting the market, but he was not enthusiastic. I also spoke to Tony Smith again, who had joined me at U-Micro shortly after I had started it. He reluctantly mentioned that he was looking for a way to get into a new area – the Internet. He needed someone to work with and, in the end, we made a deal to put together a business plan. He had an Internet access account with a company called Demon but had not been able to get it working fully. I went to a small trade show in London and came across a company called Cityscape that was offering a Windows-based package rather than PC-Dos-based and I felt that we should go that way also. On my first web browsing attempt I typed in "trees" to a search engine of the time and it took me to a university in Costa Rica!

I should add here that whilst in Warrington previously I had been interested in trees and had started a small nursery concentrating on native trees for forestry. After the move to Swansea I had bought a field on Pembrey Mountain to continue my interest. I sold the field when we left Swansea and it was that spare cash that I had available for investment. I had also been putting the research I had done into a book *British Native Trees* but had not finished it when we left Swansea.

U-NET Ltd

So we agreed to go into business with 50% each of U-Net Limited. I invested all the spare cash I had as share capital and he matched that. In addition Tony loaned the company money and managed to arrange an overdraft with no guarantees with HSBC. Tony was key to a number of early decisions. I said that I would not be able to technically set up the service and said that we had to employ someone. We advertised and I was leaning towards one guy, but Tony plumped for another guy who was extremely enthusiastic. He was just finishing university but a bit intense and was called Adrian. This turned out to be a brilliant choice. We had envisioned bringing in consultants from Daresbury Labs and UMIST but they were hardly needed. The other crucial decision regarded the computer hardware – the server. Tony asked what the established Internet services (i.e. at this time in the universities) were using and the answer was Sun Micro servers. I had my doubts about using Windows anyway (and remember that, at the time, Bill Gates had deemed the Internet just a fad). The server we were recommended to order by our consultants was a SPARC 10 but, as we ordered, the model was upgraded to SPARC 20 at the same price. The choice meant that Adrian could use existing open-source software for each of the applications – news, mail, web.

The company was formed in June 1994 and we got the hardware in September, including our first router. We got a minute office at Warrington Business Park and had 16 telephone lines installed for incoming Internet calls. We opted to get our Internet connection – 64K – from a company based in Kent called EUnet, an offshoot of the university. We could have piggy-backed off a company in Manchester called the Manchester Host that had a connection but felt that, although costing less, it would leave us dependent on a local competitor (if they ever got the message about the Internet's potential). While Adrian set up the server and router I worked on the business aspects. I produced our first sets of leaflets. I also set up two databases. One for enquiries, and one for customers. They both took a lot of work. I also decided on the products we should launch over the first year or so. EasyOneIP was our dial-up product and had a quite a few innovative features. IP stands for Internet Protocol. EasyTwoIP was our web-hosting product, EasyThreeIP was to be launched later using ISDN access and EasyFourIP was to be our leased line product. There was an "Introduction to the Internet" leaflet, and one each for EasyOneIP and EasyTwoIP. These both included joining forms. I decided to make EasyOneIP competitive with a £12 per month offer (a bit more than Demon) or a £100 pa offer (which was cheaper than Demon). The pricing structure was to make a major contribution to the success of the business because about half of the orders were for annual accounts, which meant as it took off we had cash to support investment.

We launched the product with PR and advertising at the end of November and we were able to ship the first orders just towards the end of December. The SPARC choice paid off in another way. It ran without crashing for about 3 months, whereas competitors using PCs were notoriously unreliable. We were also at a good point regarding modem technology and were one of the first to offer 33.6KBs connections.

We had looked around and had teamed up with a company called Psion-Dacom. When approached for quotes for modems they were very enthusiastic. Their MD had just come back from a trip to the USA. We ordered 16 modems at a good price and also agreed to sell modems to customers. They agreed to market our Internet service with their modems. The very few earlier competitors – Demon and Cityscape – had to upgrade their equipment to compete or offer slower service. They were invested in equipment from a company called US Robotics, which offered rack-mounted modems.

The first orders came in at the beginning of December and we just about had everything ready. Customers got a pack consisting of a joining letter, a manual and a floppy disk. We more or less insisted that customers used the disk to install the service and this drastically reduced the number of support calls. We would get calls on a Friday afternoon demanding immediate connection and saying they could set it all up themselves without help. This tended to be a disaster. Orders were evenly split between monthly and annual accounts and between cash (cheques) and credit cards. We had been given a card terminal but there was a waiting period before we could use it. Each order had a record sheet printed out and we put into a folder by date and month order. Quite a bit of cash had come in during December and, by the end of January, we were able to use the credit card machine.

There were very few non-academic websites and so I published a few including www.british-trees.com based on my planned book. It was later given to the Woodland Trust and the content absorbed into their wider website.

We met our sales forecast for the first 6 months by the end of January so it was clear that we had a potential success on our hands and I was very busy with taking orders and dealing with enquiries and Adrian was doing the support whilst maintaining the service. He had to type every user into the technical databases by hand. I made a rule that every day the sales material for enquiries and packs for joiners went in the post that day. No sitting on enquiries. Sales statistics (enquiries, joiners and later leavers and rejoiners) were produced each day. The business park had a postal service set up for tenants and that was a big help.

It was a big moment the day after sending out the first pack – waiting for the first customer to dial in and get connected. The phone call would connect to the modem and it would chirp away and finally get connected. The second day we had a first occurrence of two customers connecting at once. After that it became routine.

We had to make decisions pretty quickly about premises and staff. Two people came aboard – Colin Smith, Tony's son, and a guy called Keith. Colin had been involved in corporate finance but was between jobs and Tony asked him to come in to help by taking phone calls. He was put in an extra unit just down the corridor. He was asked to see what he could come up with in his area of expertise but the calls came in thick and fast and he never had the opportunity. Keith was one of the first customers and had been helping Adrian with some of the technical issues, so he was an obvious choice for recruitment when we realised the need. He moved into the original unit with me and Adrian. We very quickly recruited a salesman to work alongside Colin Smith.

I was doing the accounts and cash (as well as working on new leaflets and more advertising etc.). Each day I would sort out the cheques ready to take to the bank and process the credit cards. The paper system was organised so that each day of the month I processed the new orders for that day and, after the first month, the monthly recurring subscriptions. I just used a date stamp onto each customer sheet to record the transaction and put the total cash for the day into the cash book. I was soon spending an hour a day processing the credit cards, so we employed a bookkeeper to do that and other bookkeeping work.

Rapid Expansion

It was clear that we would very soon need to increase the capacity of our service and some serious financial decisions loomed. Fortunately, our pricing structure meant that we were very cash positive (excluding capital expenditure). Whilst I researched our options for better connectivity for our service I asked our provider, EUnet, if we could increase the capacity of our connection to them to 128Kbps. They were very reluctant to do so. They saw the main market as leased-line connections to businesses and organisations and saw the dial-up as a bit-player in the Internet market. But they realised that as our connectivity grew we would be able to compete with them for that market also. There was another issue here – the existing providers, who all had lines to the Internet in the USA, had just created an Internet exchange point in London called LINX. It meant that traffic did not have to go via the USA (and expensive connections to the USA) when the traffic was between UK users. If we were to grow and be seen as a serious provider we had to join LINX. A condition of joining at that time was that you had to have your own Internet connection to the USA.

The main US Internet company offering connections to overseas customers was called UUNet (this was to cause some confusion later – at the time we started they had been mainly called AlterNet). I negotiated with them and decided to go for a 128K line to them and a 64K line to LINX. Because we had to have the US connection before joining LINX I asked EUnet if they would allow us to retain our line to them until we were able to join LINX ourselves and to send our UK traffic to LINX via themselves.

A stroke of luck then intervened. UUnet did not have any available capacity on their router in Virginia on the East Coast but offered to connect us to their router in California at the same price. At that time a very large percentage of all Internet traffic was to the western USA where Internet usage was highest. We were advertising (whole pages by mid-1995) in a magazine called *Internet* and they ran a speed test on the Internet providers they listed in their directory. The test consisted of pinging a number of important websites including quite a number in California. Of course, as soon as the new line was up and running we jumped to the top of the listing and even retained it for quite a few months, greatly increasing our rate of growth.

We had one funny incident – the magazine phoned to tell us that we were the top provider for the third month running. I was just finalising the advert for the same issue of the magazine and we had time to add a prominent sticker saying "Top Provider again – June 1995". The other advertisers protested loudly about this and, after that, the magazine only released info on the ratings after the magazine went to press.

Our Internet capacity was one side of the expansion equation – the other being increasing our number of phone lines and modems. The Psion-Dacom modems were small boxes each with power, phone and Ethernet connections. Heading for hundreds of lines they were no solution, but we were reluctant to go for the obsolete USRobotics equipment. Adrian and Keith had been to a telecoms exhibition in Birmingham and said that we should look at another solution altogether from a US company called Ascend. The technology was all digital including the phone lines and each box could handle 32 phone calls at once. The boxes were expensive though – £30K plus. There was a local supplier in Warrington that we looked at but we were put in touch with a company down in Reading called BTN. I had several meetings with the MD – Ken Baynton – and they were very switched on to the potential of the Internet and wanted our business. They came up with a favourable deferred payment deal and we plumped for them. This then meant that our phone lines had to change from ordinary phone line to digital (ISDN30). They were very expensive from BT. However the local cable company, Nynex, was interested. They also saw the potential and did us a good deal – which also included putting a cabinet into the business park with fibre optic connections.

The final problem we had to solve at this time was our own customer data system. As indicated, it was part computerised but with a manual billing system. (i.e. someone keying in each credit card detail). One mistake I had made was to set up a separate database for EasyoneIP and EasytwoIP. I should have found more time and had a series of separate tables for services and customer details. I used a database system called Paradox. I cast around and a guy called Adrian Whitely (one of the U-Micro customers and then someone who did custom applications for businesses for us) expressed interest. He had worked for North-West Water and then gone on his own as a computer consultant. Crucially, he was very experienced with Paradox. We needed the existing databases merged and tidied up, we needed it to become multiuser, to send data to the servers and, crucially, we needed it to automatically generate the billing and send the credit card data directly to the bank. All these things were possible with Paradox and, after about three months' work, we had a new system operational.

So, with these four innovations U-NET successfully negotiated a pretty hazardous business situation involving immediate capacity and growth potential. I think that quite a lot of the competitors that had sprung up in the six months after we started failed at this point or were stunted.

Growth in subscriber numbers continued and we added a further unit in the business park. It was not long before decisions had to be made again about capacity. We kept the original unit with the equipment in and the one next door with the support team, but got a single much larger unit on the first floor. We just added more Ascend boxes and lines and larger Internet connections to increase the capacity of the service.

Although I had produced all the first leaflets and set the pattern for all subsequent ones I called in Roy Partington to design future leaflets and had a dedicated in-house person to work with him. The blue plus black print leaflets were replaced with full colour as were the adverts and we managed to convey a professional and friendly image. Tony had emphasised that we were a service business and that providing a good service and building a reputation were key to success in the business.

During the first six months or so I had continued to try and keep Cardio Carbon on the road and, with the agreement of the other directors, had taken a minimum salary. However progress had been painfully slow and eventually we had a titanium prototype valve produced. It had not proved possible to get a good carbon coating and I basically said we had to stop the project. I started taking a proper (but not large) salary from U-NET instead and was able to devote all my time to the business.

From the beginning of getting U-NET technically running we had had some contact with the University of Manchester Computing Centre, which ran the college's Internet service. I had liaised with the head of department. We wanted to promote the Internet in the north of England. They had space in their computer room for equipment after the retirement of their mainframe computers. They wanted to rent the space for Internet use and we agreed that it would be a very good idea to create a northern rival to LINX. After a number of meetings of interested ISPs in the area a plan was agreed and I became the chairman of MANAP (Manchester Network Access Point).

The name MINX had already been taken by an opportunistic person. The exchange point got going based in their computer space and grew gradually. I think overall it helped to make Manchester something of an Internet business hub.

The next major event arose when JANET – the UK academic network – decided to offer its customers – i.e. university departments – a dial-up service. They declined to do it themselves and offered the project to the private sector. Our Manchester contact was on the committee overseeing the contest and we were shortlisted with two others. After various meetings we were selected to offer the JANET dial-up service.

As part of the contract it was agreed that we could peer with the JANET network directly in Manchester, the argument being that this would help the experience of their users. Of course we were able to advertise the fact that we were the only ISP with a direct connection to JANET. The guy that handled the negotiations for MANAP left their service and managed to get VC funding to set up a new building to host Internet infrastructure and servers in Manchester. The university were very upset about this and, although he had asked me for our support, I decided that it was best for U-NET to retain the connection with the university rather that getting into bed with a rival. The guy who left called his company Telecity and, after the success of their hosting centre in Manchester, expanded the company greatly with buildings in London and then all over Europe. I don't know how much he made out of it, but it could have been substantial.

Major Relocation

Our next move was to take over a building on Birchwood Boulevard, Warrington, where there were a lot of new business units. It was a big risk to take, but we were simply growing too fast to take more units at Warrington Business Park and run an efficient business. The industry was also starting to grow up and we needed to think of a more professional image. We took over the front half of a building at first. We knew that the move could prove difficult, but did as much as we could in advance. We had to get the telecoms into the building and get ahead on our equipment needs so that there was duplicate equipment if needed. We set up multiple leased lines between the old and new sites so that equipment could communicate very quickly. Colin took care of the fitting out of the building and we had a machine room set up including channelling into the concrete floor for multiple power points, overhead trunking for cables, automatic fire suppression, entrance security, back-up generator etc. We got rid of all the second-hand furniture and leased stylish Danish desks and tables.

The events of the move and just after changed my attitude to the business. It had been hard work but a lot of fun. Now it involved a lot of money and serious risks. The first disaster was that we were unable to get the dial-up service working for about 3 days. We had warned all the users and started the changeover on a weekend. We took a lot of flak for this and I had visions of the business being severely damaged. Surprisingly, once things started working again everybody settled down.

We had a simple telephone system for voice calls at the business park. In the new premises a complex switching system was installed. It allowed us to do all sorts of sophisticated things with calls, including generating statistics such as how long people were in a queue etc. I used to have the post opened each morning and put on my desk to check it. A couple of months after the move, the monthly telephone bill came in and showed an £8000 charge for a couple of days with calls to Sri Lanka etc. I took the bill down to Colin and asked him to urgently sort it out. The next monthly bill showed over £100,000 of charges and would have been enough to severely damage the business as we had no financial resources apart from the cash flow and a lot of that was going into capital equipment. I took it down to Colin and, as he read it, he turned white. He said that he had passed the problem to one of the engineers but obviously nothing had been done. It turned out that the new system came with a default password that had become known to criminals in Manchester and calls were being made out of hours to our switch (a local call) and then being routed all over the world at our cost.

When we started, calls to us from Liverpool, Manchester (and Warrington) were charged as local calls. This meant that we had a very large attractive customer base almost as big as London and, of course, at first competition was minimal. We had customers from all over the UK as well, even though they had to call long distance. Eventually the telephone companies started to get interested in this Internet traffic and it became possible to call us using 0845 numbers from anywhere in the UK at a local call rate. What I hadn't realised was that the telephone company that handled the final delivery of the call to the customer got paid a credit from the initiating call telco.

This in a way explained why Nynex was prepared to invest in service to us. In fact, for a time, we were Nynex's largest customer. We were starting to gear up to take advantage of this and negotiate deals to take a share of the call revenue when we had our switch disaster. Our telco for voice calls was Cable and Wireless (C&W). They mitigated the bill to some extent by discounting their own calls, but they owed money to the overseas telcos terminating the calls. We eventually had to do a deal with C&W by which we continued to use them as a main telco supplier, including our Internet access, and paid down the bill over a period. This severely limited our ability to get much better deals.

Sale of U-NET

The effect of these two situations was to make me apprehensive about the future – I owned a substantial share of a fast-growing hi-tech business but was taking just an ordinary salary and no contributions towards a pension. I negotiated with Tony first of all to get a bonus to allow me to pay off our mortgage. Then, with his agreement, we started to put out feelers to either sell or float the business. An early competitor based in London – Easynet – had done an early flotation on AIM, but seemed to have floundered, after not growing very much and putting effort into convincing large corporates to use them for complex database-driven websites. They did turn tack around this time and got themselves a telephone licence and installed a telephone exchange so that they could keep all the termination revenue. However, their lacklustre performance did make flotation for us at that time look difficult. So we started looking round for a buyer and even had an offer from Easynet, though this was way below our requirements. We set a figure that we could accept and kept on looking until that was met.

A further consequence of the problems on the changeover was that I lost confidence in Adrian's ability to manage the increasingly complex systems and the team he managed. Maybe it had been unfair to put so much responsibility on his shoulders. He had worked as a team with Keith who was a more experienced character. Initially we looked to recruit a new technical manager and even interviewed someone who had been the chief tech guy at U-Micro at one point. In the end, we decided to put Keith in overall charge of the technical aspects of the business.

When I started in business with U-Micro in 1979 it was motivated by my desire to start my own business. I felt it was something that I could make a success of and I would enjoy being my own boss. I had worked for people and companies that had various degrees of competence and felt, on the whole, I could do better. Of course, I had an awful lot to learn and, to some extent, my knowledge was only really up to the job when I started U-NET in 1994. So money was not the main objective when I started in business at first. However, when I started U-NET making money *was* my aim. As we progressed I kept a file of "legal documents" – things like leases, contracts etc. under my control. This proved invaluable when we did sell.

The search for a buyer went up a gear towards the end of 1997 and we appointed an investment firm to search for a buyer. ISPs were becoming hot property. We prepared business plans and projections and kept them updated. The business continued to expand rapidly and, from a half of a building on Birchwood Boulevard, we took over another building and then all of the building we had originally moved to. We doubled the amount of machine room in the original building and moved out sales and accounts.

The billing system using Paradox was becoming difficult to expand and we wanted to start to do things that are common now, such as customers themselves being able to access the system, change passwords and order new products. This was innovative at the time, so the decision was made to move to a custom-developed system using the Oracle database system. At the time there was no commercially available alternative. The system had to integrate all the billing and customer details along with external services such as domain registrations and, of course, the credit card processing companies. We ended up with a team of three or four people working full-time on the project and eventually changed over to it without major hassle. Development continued however as more functionality was demanded by sales and support.

The strong emphasis on the database system partly arose after a meeting we had with a potential reseller of our services. The company was the largest mobile phone reseller at the time (Carphone Warehouse) and we met their financial director to discuss. They didn't really grasp what an Internet network was, equating it to the way mobile phone systems work. However he put down their continued success to their investment whilst growing in a system to handle the customer data and mobile phone accounts. Other players faded away as they were unable to cope with the growth without such as system. So we definitely took this on board.

The management had been expanded by then and we had a full-time accountant with a dedicated team handling the accounts, while also dealing with customers on accounts queries. We employed a sales manager to work with the sales team and, parallel to the telesales team, employed a reseller manager to get us business from computer consultants (I think having a reseller product was something of an innovation for ISPs at the time). We also employed a marketing manager and increased the marketing team to two additional staff.

At the end of 1997 I had been working to increase U-NETs reach and potential by seeking to cooperate with ISPs in the USA and Europe. I had attended conferences of various Internet bodies to facilitate this. I felt that we could expand our business not by setting up subsidiaries in other countries but by selling access to our growing international Internet network to smaller ISPs.

Towards the beginning of 1998 we got into discussions with a company called VIAnetworks, a VC funded start-up planning to create a pan-European ISP. I had been in touch with a USA start-up that had the same genesis a bit earlier and that had achieved quite a bit of success. They had passed our details to VIA.

The negotiations to sell the business became protracted and we had meetings with many potential buyers, mostly international telcos. In the end, VIA came up with an acceptable offer and we then embarked on a seemingly never-ending saga. I think that this is not unusual, but in their case they had very little understanding of the business and had employed consultants for almost all the functions that the management needed to get to grips with. There was a danger that all they would use us for was to increase their own knowledge. They did, however, have something of a deadline to get the money they had raised invested and came under time pressure to find suitable businesses.

I remember that they sent a technical guy to evaluate the business, who was totally out of touch with what we were doing. After a day's meetings I arranged for him to go to Chester for a sightseeing day, which he quite enjoyed. The contracts passed back and forth between our lawyers for months. They had a template for contracts, which was very general and put us through all sorts of irrelevant hoops particularly regarding environmental protection. We didn't produce or process anything tangible – produce waste water or effluent waste water, or emissions. My faith in lawyers (well, US lawyers) went down quite a bit and, on a number of occasions, I was told outright lies by their lawyer – i.e. contradicting what we already had in writing.

We had also started the process for a flotation on AIM but stopped after the initial offer from VIA.

I think that it is true to say that the management of the business suffered in this period. There were things that we should have moved forward on that we didn't do. I did not want to let the staff know what was going on, although it was obvious with all the meetings that something was occurring. By then I had a large office with a conference room on the first floor and that part of the building was shared entirely with technical people – database development and network management (the NOC – Network Operations Centre) who were probably not that observant of comings and goings. It did, however, come out towards the end of the process.

The guy we were dealing with was called Mike S. and he was rushing around Europe making deals. I was told by Colin that one of the visitors from VIA had been asked by the taxi driver taking him back to the airport what he was doing in the UK. He had replied "We are buying that company!!" However, the taxi had been booked for him by one of our staff – whose boyfriend was the taxi driver. So everybody heard about that. I later mentioned this to Mike Simmons and he was not amused. I found out somewhat later that he had been the visitor. He may have thought that I was devious and pretending to not know it was him, but we didn't really get on after the acquisition.

In the end it all came together. We had produced a stack of A4 ring-binders of contract and supporting documentation and a completion date was agreed. We met in Manchester at the solicitors and signed all the paperwork. We waited for a call around lunchtime for the other party to confirm we had signed everything and then waited for the money to be transferred. Actually, the deal was half cash on completion and half loan notes to be paid in 12 months, which I was not too happy with. As it came to the end of the day, we were told that there had been some hold-up on the money. All the documents were put into escrow and we went home. We eventually had a call around lunchtime the following day that the payment had been received by our solicitors and the deal was actually completed.

We visited my parents in Bedford that weekend to celebrate with a meal out. At that time I asked my mother whether I should share some of my good fortune with my siblings and she said no. Some years later she asked me how much I had got for the business and was very shocked when I told her.

Part of the agreement was that Colin and I had twelve months renewable service contracts (at quite a lot higher salary than before). I had said that I would not stay after the 12 months and my main task was to recruit a new managing director for the business. Colin had hoped to stay on for a while longer. Colin had been having trouble with his back and in January 1999 had to go into hospital for an operation. So it meant for the next few months I was full time running the business. I interviewed various MD candidates that had been preselected by an agency appointed by VIA and eventually settled on someone. I had also been appointed MD of VIAnetworks UK Ltd and made a half-hearted effort to coordinate things for them in the UK. However, it was a bit of a non-job as they had no real vision for the business.

At the time of the acquisition we had been asked to produce a detailed business plan. A few months after the sale I had a call from Mike S. asking what our plans for the business were. I was a bit flabbergasted and pointed out that a detailed plan had already been presented and we were waiting on the go ahead to implement it. Silence! Actually, at the time of the sale a business called Freeserve had been launched, which did not require a subscription and was based on running the business from the call revenue, income from their website, and charging premium rates for support calls. It grew very rapidly and we looked at competing with them. Maybe we would have done so, making our existing dial-up service our premium product. VIA took over a much smaller company in Reading at the same time as us and they did launch such a service through some contacts they had and it did expand rapidly without making money. The deal they had with VIA however included an earn-out clause based on increasing turnover during the first year of ownership and VIA ended up having to make large extra payments!

The last year before the sale was stressful and I was glad I got out. VIA floated into the dotcom boom and I did invest some of my money as a bit of a punt, figuring that they could do well in spite of their management! ADSL technology was just starting to arrive and I had been planning for us to start to offer broadband, including installing our own equipment into telephone exchanges. Unlike dial-up, there was no equivalent of the local dial-up area (i.e. for us Warrington, Liverpool, and Manchester) so equipment eventually would have to go into every exchange. BT eventually started to offer large "pipes" that we could have plugged into to get national coverage, with us being able to cherrypick the exchanges we wanted to install our own equipment in.

Once the MD was installed and after induction it became obvious to me that two of us could not run the business. I had to let him get on with it. He really reported to VIA rather than me and I had less and less to do. We had started to get our own telecoms licence prior to the sale (so that we could get our own call revenue) and I continued with that. I attended overseas conferences to fly the flag but over the last part of the year I was just treading water and didn't really have much I could do.

I finished at the end of November 1999 and left without any kind of fanfare.

My Life Part 2

Early on in writing this memoir, I decided that leaving U-NET would be the appropriate time to stop. Thanks for reading!

Scientific Papers

Metal Halogen Stretching Modes in the Far-infrared Spectra of Octahedral Transition Metal (II) complexes containing Halogen Bridges, M. Goldstein and W. D. Unsworth, Inorg. Nucl. Chem. Letters,1970, 6, 25;

The Far-infrared Spectra (450 – 80 cm-1) of Octahedral Halogen-bridged Transition Metal (II) Complexes, Inorganica Chim Acta, 1970,4, 342;

Infrared and Raman Spectra (3500 – 70 cm-1) and Mossbauer spectra of some pyrazine complexes of stannic halides, Spectrochim. Acta, 1971, 27a, 1055;

The Vibrational Spectra of Dimethyltin Difluoride and some Related Compounds, J. Chem. Soc. (A), 1971, 2121;

Raman (300 – 10 cm-1) and further far-infrared (100 – 20 cm-1) spectra of octahedral halogen-bridged transition metal (II) complexes, Spectrochim. Acta, 1972, 28a, 1107;

The far-infrared spectra of dihalogenotetra(pyridine) metal (II) complexes and related six-co-ordinate compounds containing terminal metal halogen bonds, Spectrochim. Acta, 1972, 28a, 127;

The far-infrared and Raman spectra of some complexes of cadmium dihalides with pyridine, pyrazine, dioxan, and aniline, J. Mol. Struct., 1972, 14, 451;

Far-infrared Spectra of Bis(pyrazine) complexes of Transition Metal (II) Halides. The Crystal and Molecular Structure or

Dichlorobis(pyrazine)cobalt (II).P. W. Careck, M. Goldstein, E. M. McPartlin, and W. D. Unsworth Chem. Comm., 1971, 1634.

Infrared Spectra, Electronic Spectra, and Magnetic Properties of Dihalogenobis(pyrazine) complexes of Cobalt(II) and Nickel (II); a Structural Re-assignment, M. Goldstein, F. B. Taylor and W. D. Unsworth, J. Chem. Soc. (Dalton), 1972, 418.

Vibrational spectra of bis-pyridine and complexes of mercury (II) halides. A literature correction and structural implications, R. M. Barr, M. Goldstein, and W. D. Unsworth J. Cryst. Mol. Structure, 1974, 4, 165.

Vibrational Spectra of some heavy metal tetrafluorides in the solid state, M. Goldstein, R. J. Hughes, and W. D. Unsworth, Spectrochim Acta, 1975, 31a, 621.

Various Business Trips
– as per postcards I sent to my parents.

When	From	Comments	
1972	Rheims	Intl Raman Conf	Varian
1975	Warsaw	Cary seminar	
1976	Amsterdam	ECOG	VG
11/12/1976	Karlsruhe, Germany		
1976	Moscow	Britnauchpribor	
1977	Caracas, Mexico City		
1977	Tokyo, Seoul, Taipei		
1977	Brussels		
1977	Bangkok, Tokyo, Hong Kong		
1977	Finland		
1977	Halifax, Toronto, Saskatoon, Vancouver		
1977	Lerwick, Shetlands	On way to Dounreay	
18/5/1978	Oak Ridge, Tennessee		
21/7/1978	Washington, US		
2/9/1978	Brisbane, Australia	ICOG	
27/9/1978	Zurich, Switzerland		
29/11/1978	Bombay, Beijing, Urumchi		
12/2/1979	Anchorage, Tokyo	On way to Tokyo	

When	From	Comments
3/5/1979	Vancouver, Seattle, San Francisco	
16/10/1981	Germany, Belgium, France	U-Micro
21/4/1982	Zurich, Vienna	
7/11/1986	Atlantic City, US	
17/2/1988	Basel	
9/8/1988	San Francisco	
19/1/1991	Minneapolis, US	Cardio Carbon
19/11/1991	Vancouver, Singapore	
5/2/1997	Washington, San Francisco	U-NET
19/8/1997	San Francisco	
25/5/1998	Hamburg, Frankfurt	
21/7/1998	Geneva	
5/4/1999	Washington	VIA networks
17/6/1999	San Jose	

www.ingramcontent.com/pod-product-compliance
Lightning Source LLC
Chambersburg PA
CBHW060301050426
42448CB00009B/1709